Vegan Cooking for One

By the same author:

Easy Vegan Cooking
The Tofu Cookbook

Vegan Cooking for One

Leah Leneman

thorsons

Thorsons
An Imprint of HarperCollins*Publishers*
77–85 Fulham Palace Road
Hammersmith, London W6 8JB

The website address is www.thorsonselement.com

and *Thorsons* are trademarks of
HarperCollins*Publishers* Limited

Published by Thorsons 2000
Originally published as *The Single Vegan* 1989

13 14 12

A catalogue record for this book
is available from the British Library

ISBN-13 978-0-7225-3923-1
ISBN-10 0-7225-3923-1

Printed and bound in Great Britain by
Martins The Printers Limited, Berwick upon Tweed

Contents

Introduction

Most cookery books, vegan or otherwise, are aimed at a family of four, and dividing ingredients to make them suitable for one is often not feasible. Of course, the same dish could be eaten four nights running, but who wants to do that? Or you could freeze the remainder, but only certain types of dishes are suitable for freezing, and it still means eating leftovers. Also, many of the recipes found in ordinary cookery books involve a degree of time and effort which may be appropriate for the preparation of a meal for a family, a partner or friends, but does not seem worth the bother when cooking just for oneself.

It is not just the amount of time needed to cook a meal that counts either; the planning involved is often the most off-putting thing. Yet to stick to the same tried and true recipes day after day is very boring indeed – no wonder so many companies are now producing convenience meals for one person! Some of them aren't bad at all, but they rarely match up to a home-cooked meal, and they are *much* more expensive.

This book is designed to overcome those obstacles to cooking for one. Each week begins with a Sunday lunch. Dinner on Sunday night is slightly more time-consuming than on other nights of the week, as this is likely to be the one day of the week when some extra time can be afforded. And for this meal a dessert recipe is also provided. From Monday to Friday the assumption is that lunch will be had out. The recipes for evening meals are all quick and easy to prepare, while at the same time providing lots of variety. For Saturday a lunch recipe is given, but the likelihood is that one night a week a break from cooking will be desired, and a meal had at a restaurant or with friends. By the end of any week all perishable ingredients will have been used up, and, to make the planning as simple as possible, a shopping list precedes each week's menus.

The book does not, however, have to be utilized in the way described above; it can be used in the same way as any other cookery book, since each recipe stands on its own. Nor does it have to be used for single people only; ingredients are far more easily doubled, or even quadrupled, than halved or quartered. And although the recipes are all vegan – for even vegans not living alone may have to prepare separate meals for themselves – the menus aim to be interesting and varied enough to satisfy vegans, lacto-vegetarians and omnivores.

Breakfast

Given the importance of starting the day with something nourishing, one can't really *not* mention breakfast, although no recipes are provided. Vegans have plenty of choice these days with dairy-free mueslis and the like (however, some cereals are not suitable because they are fortified with an animal-derived vitamin D). Porridge is a nice starter for a cold winter's morning; or for a savoury hot breakfast, scrambled tofu, or thinly sliced and fried tofu, fits the bill nicely. Breakfast is one meal that causes no problems to single vegans.

Lunch

As indicated in the introduction above, the assumption is that the majority of people using this book will not be concerned with preparing a daily lunch. Every vegetarian restaurant now caters for vegans, and even non-vegetarian restaurants often have vegan salads and/or baked potatoes, etc. Eating lunch out in many parts of the country is no longer a problem for a vegan.

If daily restaurant lunches are not easily affordable then it is easy enough to bring a packed lunch in to work. There are an increasing number of vegan pâtés and spreads for sandwiches, as well as vegan biscuits. A number of the Saturday and Sunday lunch dishes in this book – such as spreads, salads and the like – could be taken to work for midday lunches as well.

For those who do not go out to work but lunch at home, the weekend lunch recipes could be used. A healthy alternative is simply a daily mixed salad, with differing ingredients and accompaniments for variety. There are also many more packet soups and convenience foods like tofu burgers which are vegan these days.

There are some people who prefer to eat a large midday meal and only a light supper in the evening; the daily recipes could of course be used for a midday meal and the above suggestions be utilized for the evening meal.

Quantities

The most useful kitchen implement for a single person is a dieter's scale: using one of those you can weigh as little as ¼ oz (5g), which is invaluable for small quantities.

Many cookery books insist that imperial and metric measurements should not be mixed. As far as I am concerned, anyone using this book should feel free to mix imperial, metric and even American measurements to their heart's content. The recipes are intended to be robust enough not to require precision, which is why, in the newer recipes particularly, I have often suggested a range of quantities of a particular ingredient, to give maximum flexibility.

The weekly menus are intended to use up all ingredients that would otherwise spoil and are based on standard-sized cans. When using half a can of beans or other vegetables in one recipe, the other half should be transferred to a glass or plastic container and refrigerated until needed later in the week. In the UK tofu is usually found in 8 or 10 oz packets, and I have therefore used this amount as the basis of a week's menus, but there are various recipes calling for frozen tofu, so if a larger quantity is purchased the remainder can be frozen.

Vegetables

Recipes in standard cookery books often call for 1 onion or 2 onions, which is a bit meaningless since one can buy onions as small as 2 oz (55g) or as large as 8 oz (225g). When I specify a 'small onion' I mean 2–4 oz (55–115g). It is usually quite easy to find onions of this size, but if your local shop only has large ones you can chop off this amount, wrap the remainder in clingfilm and store it in a fridge until onion is required for another recipe. Garlic cloves are also very variable in size; if the only kind available seems large enough to flavour a dish for four people then this too can be quartered with the remainder wrapped in clingfilm and stored in the fridge (though it's a good idea to put an extra plastic bag round it to keep the fridge from reeking of garlic). When a recipe calls for a small carrot I mean 2–3 oz (55–85g); a small green pepper is about 6 oz (170g), a small courgette (zucchini) 3–4 oz (85–115g).

Certain vegetables are more awkward for one person to use, for example cauliflower. I have tried always to incorporate such vegetables into more than one recipe in a week's menu so that you are not left with a large chunk of it in the fridge with no idea what to do with it. Celery is a particular nuisance I find because a little of it goes very nicely in some dishes but as a whole head is difficult to use up. Spring onions (scallions) are arguably in the same category except that they will keep in the fridge for some weeks.

I know that some single people prefer to keep a stock of frozen vegetables, but I can't see the point when it is easier (and a lot cheaper) to buy half a dozen fresh Brussels sprouts than to pull out the same number of frozen ones. The only exception I make is green beans or peas when they are out of season.

Pulses

Many of the recipes in this book call for canned beans. The reason is simply that unless you have a pressure cooker, cooking dried beans takes an awfully long time, which may be acceptable if you are cooking for a family but not for a single person. Unlike vegetables, which lose vitamins (not to mention flavour) when canned, protein is not lost in the canning process, so canned beans are as nutritious as freshly cooked ones. Admittedly they can be high in salt content, and some British brands add sugar as well, but it is easy enough to rinse the beans off before using them. There is no doubt, however, that canned beans work out a lot more expensive than dried ones, so if money is more important than time then by all means use home-cooked beans instead of canned ones: a small can or half a large one is equivalent to 2 oz (55g) dried beans, and an ordinary can to about 4 oz (115g).

Butter (lima) beans and red kidney beans are available in small cans, which obviates the need to use the other half of a can later in the week. All other beans are available only in larger cans so I have used them in two recipes in the relevant week. The beans not used in the first recipe should not be left in the can but transferred to a jar and refrigerated until required.

Certain pulses – e.g., lentils, aduki beans, split peas, and black-eyed peas – are not readily available in cans and are quite quick to cook so in those cases the dried varieties are called for.

Salads

There are basically two types of salad. (Well, three if you count the typical British salad of limp lettuce leaves, a slice of tomato and one of cucumber, topped with something sliced, with vinegary salad cream over it, but anyone reading this book is unlikely to think of such a thing when talking of salads.) The first kind of real salad is a meal in itself. Such salads feature as recipes for some weekend lunches.

The second kind is a side salad, i.e., it accompanies a dish in the same way as cooked vegetables. Many of the recipes in this book would be nice accompanied by a salad even when this is not specified. It is easy enough to make a salad for one person. Some lettuce or cress, a small grated carrot, a few sliced button mushrooms – that alone makes a very palatable salad even if there is nothing else to add to it, and if there is celery, a few spring onions (scallions), green pepper or other leftovers in the fridge, so much the better. A few chopped black olives really zing up a salad. The easiest dressing for this type of salad is a little oil – especially virgin olive oil – mixed with a little cider vinegar or lemon juice, perhaps with a pinch of mustard, and any additional seasoning desired. It is useful to have a ready-made vinaigrette dressing handy, but unfortunately most supermarket ones are made with malt vinegar which is anything but nutritious (or even *nice*). Fortunately, more wholefood shops are beginning to stock good ones.

Herbs and Spices

It has become easier to obtain fresh herbs of late, and some people grow their own. Obviously fresh herbs have a wonderful flavour, and anyone who has access to them will certainly want to use them, but the majority will find it much easier to keep a variety of dried herbs in stock. When herbs are called for in recipes it is dried herbs that are meant.

As far as spices are concerned, although there is nothing intrinsically wrong with the mixture of spices which go to make up 'curry powder', far more interesting variations of flavour can be obtained by using the spices themselves. For the best flavour, coriander and cumin seeds are much better bought whole and ground in a small pestle and mortar when required. I realize such a suggestion may seem surprising in a book which is aimed at simple and quick recipes, but the average time required to grind a teaspoonful of spice cannot be more than about five seconds, and it is especially beneficial when cooking for one simply because these spices are likely to be stored for a long time, since only a little is required for any one dish, and if bought already powdered then much of the flavour will gradually be lost.

Rice and Pasta

If used straight from the packet, brown rice generally takes about 45 minutes to cook, which makes it less than ideal for a really quick meal. However, if it is covered with boiling water in the morning and left to soak all day then it will only take about 20–25 minutes. (The method is to drain the soaking water, cover the rice with water about a ¼-inch (5mm) over the top and a little salt, bring to the boil, lower heat, cover pan and simmer until all the water is absorbed.) This is all very well for well-organized people but rather annoying if you arrive home in the evening to realize you have forgotten the soaking step. There are now several brands of brown rice available in supermarkets which require no soaking and take only 25 minutes or so to cook. The method with these types of rice is different: the rice is covered with lots of boiling water and simmered uncovered before being drained and more hot water poured over it. As the water is not all absorbed, this type of rice is not suitable for pilaus and similar dishes which require the flavouring to be incorporated into the rice. These supermarket packets also work out rather more expensive than rice bought at a wholefood shop. The best compromise may be to use the latter normally but keep the supermarket kind in stock for emergencies or when the soaking has been forgotten. I find about 3 oz (85g) wholefood shop brown rice or 2½ oz (70g) supermarket brown rice to be right for one serving.

Wholemeal (whole wheat) pasta is available now in a variety of shapes and sizes. Not all of the packets provide information on cooking time. Twelve to fifteen minutes seems to be about the average time required for most types of wholemeal (whole wheat) pasta to cook.

Most Chinese noodles are egg noodles, but Chinese shops (and some supermarkets) sell a variety of eggless noodles, some made from wheat flour and some from rice flour. Wholemeal (whole wheat) Chinese-style noodles are available at some health food stores. Most need little or no cooking, making them an ideal food for those in a hurry.

Dessert

Dessert is not a necessary part of anyone's diet, and many people are perfectly happy to end a meal with a savoury taste. Unfortunately, there are many of us brought up in such a way that a meal simply is not complete unless it ends with a sweet. For those of us in that situation all that can be done is to try and make the sweet course a healthy addition to the diet.

Fresh fruit is the most commonly suggested healthy dessert, but for die-hard sweet-toothed types, a fresh apple, pear or banana, which may be very welcome in the morning or between meals, does not constitute a real dessert. That is not to say there aren't some fresh fruits which do. In the summer months fresh strawberries, raspberries, and similar soft fruit – particularly if served with cashew or coconut cream – certainly does, also sweet melons and the like. In the winter tropical fruits like fresh pineapple or mango are definitely reserved for dessert. Another winter fruit which can be classified as a dessert is the persimmon (also called Sharon fruit). For those who have not tried this fruit, it should be eaten when it is so soft it feels almost rotten. The skin is peeled off and the inside is unbelievably sweet.

Canned fruit is not the same, of course, but there are an increasing number of varieties canned in juice rather than sugar syrup; served with cashew cream or custard made from soya milk, they can serve as a pleasant dessert as well.

Nowadays there are an increasing number of vegan sweets available, both in the UK and USA, including ready-made puddings and dairy-free ice creams. Naturally a convenience-type dessert can never be the same as a home-made one, which is why I have included sweet recipes for one in Sunday meals, when there may be extra leisure time to make them.

Staples

A shopping list precedes each week's menus, but it is assumed that certain foods will be kept permanently in the larder, and therefore those foods do not appear on weekly shopping lists. The items considered staples are the following:

HERBS

Sage	Oregano
Thyme	Bay leaves
Marjoram	Rosemary
Basil (sweet basil)	Mint

SPICES

Nutmeg
Cinnamon
Cloves
Ginger
Turmeric
Cumin
Coriander

Mustard seeds
Chilli powder or
      cayenne pepper
Paprika
Garam masala
      (a mixture of spices)

MISCELLANEOUS

Wholemeal (whole wheat) bread
Sea salt and black pepper
Garlic salt

Baking powder
Raw cane sugar
Wholemeal (whole wheat) flour
Yeast extract
Nutritional yeast flakes or powder
Soya milk
Soya cream
Soya yogurt
Cornflour (cornstarch)
Peanut butter
Bulgur wheat
Vegan Parmesan

Vegan margarine
Vegetable oil (e.g. soya
      or corn)
Extra virgin olive oil
Soya sauce
Cider vinegar
Tomato paste
Brown rice
Wholemeal (whole wheat)
      spaghetti and macaroni

Introduction to the New Edition

In the 10 years since *The Single Vegan* was published, many new vegan products have appeared on the market, and existing ones have become much more widely available. Both in the UK and USA there are vegan cream cheeses and even sour cream. The UK is better for hard cheeses, with varieties ranging from Cheshire-style to Edam-style. They do not behave quite like dairy cheese insofar as they do not brown on top of a dish under a grill (broiler) or in the oven, but they do melt very satisfactorily. In the USA most so-called non-dairy cheeses contain casein, a dairy derivative, but there are some completely vegan ones to be found. I have used hard vegan cheeses in some of the new recipes but for the sake of flexibility have not specified any particular kind. Those who have a choice can experiment and see which kind is most appealing in any particular dish. Anyone unable to find a vegan hard cheese at all can make the mixture described under 'Scalloped Tofu au Gratin' in Week 5 of Spring/Summer menus (see page 47).

Plain soya (soy) yogurt is now readily available, but anyone unable to find this can easily make it, using a commercial yogurt ferment on soya (soy) instead of dairy milk. Vegan Parmesan can easily be found in both the UK and USA and is great for Italian-style dishes. Soya (soy) cream is now readily available in the UK and makes a useful addition to the vegan larder. Sliced imitation 'chicken' and 'turkey' are also readily available, and though one wouldn't want to eat too much of them, I have used them in some new recipes to add variety and show how they can be incorporated into hot dishes rather than just sandwiches. I have also used frozen vegan 'fishless fishcakes' in a couple of recipes to show their versatility.

Apart from substitutes for dairy and meat products, other new foods have also appeared to extend the vegan range of dishes, in particular sun-dried tomatoes, both dried and in oil. Both will keep for a long time and therefore can be used in single-person recipes without needing to be used up. Fresh herbs are now much easier to find and therefore have been included in some of the new recipes. Coconut milk is delicious, but a stardard-size can is enough for four people; I have therefore used it in only one week's menus but in four separate dishes.

Another change in the last 10 years has been my realization of how useful a microwave oven can be for anyone cooking meals for one. I have suggested this as an alternative in just one of the recipes from the first edition but suggest it in several of the new recipes. ALL MICROWAVE TIMINGS ARE BASED ON A 750W OVEN.

Spring/ Summer Recipes

Week 1

Shopping list

··

VEGETABLES AND FRUIT
Spring onions (scallions)
Olives
1 small red pepper
1 lb (455g) potatoes
6 small onions
10 oz (285g) mushrooms
Capers
Spring cabbage (collards)
4 oz (115g) apricots
Garlic
1 small green pepper
1 small leek
1 small courgette (zucchini)
4 oz (115g) green beans

MISCELLANEOUS
10 oz (285g) packet smoked
   tofu
Red lentils
Vegetable suet or hard
   vegetable fat
Apple juice
15½ oz (440 g) can borlotti
   (pinto) beans
Millet
Flaked (slivered) almonds
Walnut pieces

Check that you have all the staples listed on pages xiii and xiv.

SUNDAY LUNCH *Italian Pasta Salad*

IMPERIAL/METRIC		AMERICAN
3 oz (85g)	wholemeal (whole wheat) macaroni or other pasta shape	3 oz
1	spring onion (scallion)	1
4	olives	4
½	small red pepper	½
1 slice	wholemeal (whole wheat) bread	1 slice
2 oz (55g)	smoked tofu	¼ cup
1½ tbs	olive oil	1½ tbs
1 tsp	cider vinegar	1 tsp
pinch	garlic salt	pinch
pinch	oregano	pinch
	freshly ground black pepper	

1 Cook the pasta until just tender. Drain, cool, then chill.
2 Chop the spring onion (scallion) and olives finely. Chop the red pepper. Toast the bread, then dice it. Dice the tofu. Place all these ingredients in a bowl with the cooked pasta.
3 In a cup mix the oil, vinegar, garlic salt, oregano and pepper to taste. Pour the dressing over the salad and mix it all thoroughly.

SUNDAY DINNER *Potato and Lentil Bake*

IMPERIAL/METRIC		AMERICAN
½ lb (225g)	potatoes*	½ lb
2 oz (55g)	red lentils	⅓ cup
4 fl oz (115ml)	water	½ cup
1 tbs	vegan margarine	1 tbs
1 small	onion	1 small
2 oz (55g)	mushrooms	1 cup
1½ tbs	wholemeal (whole wheat) flour	1½ tbs
1 tbs	tomato paste	1 tbs
¼ pint (140ml)	soya milk	⅔ cup
¼ tsp	basil (sweet)	¼ tsp
	freshly ground black pepper	
	spring cabbage (collards)	

1 Scrub the potatoes and cook them in lightly salted water until tender.
2 Cover the lentils with the water, add a little sea salt if desired, bring to the boil, lower the heat. Cook until the lentils are tender and the water is absorbed.
3 Melt the margarine in a pan. Chop the onion and add it to the pan. Sauté for a minute or two. Slice the mushrooms and add them to the pan. Sauté for a further 3–4 minutes.
4 Add the flour and tomato paste to the pan, and stir well. Very slowly, add the milk, stirring constantly to avoid lumps. When it is boiling and has thickened, stir in the basil and pepper to taste.
5 When the lentils are cooked, stir them into the sauce.
6 When the potatoes are cooked (if too hot to handle, rinse them under cold water), slice them thickly. Spread them out in an oven dish, and top with the sauce. Bake at 400°F (200°C) Gas Mark 6 for 15–20 minutes. Serve accompanied with lightly-steamed spring cabbage (collards).

* If preparing the whole week's menus, cook 1 lb (455g) potatoes and store half in the refrigerator.

SUNDAY DESSERT *Apricot Brown Betty*

IMPERIAL/METRIC		AMERICAN
4 oz (115g)	apricots	¼ lb
1 tbs plus additional to taste	raw cane sugar	1 tbs plus additional to taste
1 tbs	water	1 tbs
1½ oz (45g)	wholemeal (whole wheat) breadcrumbs	⅔ cup
½ oz (15g)	vegetable suet or hard vegetable fat	1 tbs
¼ tsp	cinnamon	¼ tsp

1 Chop the apricots and put them in a small pan with sugar to taste (depending on ripeness of the fruit and personal preference) and the water, and stew until tender.
2 Put the breadcrumbs in a bowl. Grate the vegetable fat and add it to the breadcrumbs. Add the sugar and the cinnamon and mix thoroughly.
3 Place half the breadcrumb mixture at the bottom of a small greased oven dish, spoon the apricots on top and then add the remainder of the breadcrumb mixture.
4 Bake at 400°F (200°C) Gas Mark 6 for about half an hour. Serve with cashew or coconut cream if desired.

MONDAY *Smoky Beans*

IMPERIAL/METRIC		AMERICAN
1 small	onion	1 small
1 small clove	garlic	1 small clove
1 tbs	vegetable oil	1 tbs
2 oz (55g)	smoked tofu	¼ cup
3 fl oz (85ml)	apple juice	⅓ cup
1 tsp	tomato paste	1 tsp
pinch	marjoram	pinch
1 small or ½ large	bay leaf	1 small or ½ large
½ x 15½ oz (440g) can	borlotti (pinto) beans	½ x 15½ oz can
½ lb (225g)	cooked potatoes	½ lb
1–2 tbs	soya milk	1–2 tbs
1 tbs	vegan margarine	1 tbs
	sea salt and freshly ground black pepper to taste	

1 Chop the onion and crush the garlic. Heat the oil in a pan and sauté the onion and garlic for 2–3 minutes.
2 Dice the tofu. Add it to the pan and sauté for a further 2–3 minutes.
3 Add the apple juice, tomato paste, marjoram and bay leaf. Bring to the boil, then lower the heat and simmer, uncovered, for about 5 minutes.
4 Add the drained beans and cook for a further 5 minutes.
5 Meanwhile, mash the potatoes in a bowl. Heat the milk and margarine in a small saucepan and add to the potatoes, along with seasoning to taste. Spoon the mashed potatoes into a heatproof dish and place under the grill (broiler) until thoroughly heated.
6 Remove the bay leaf from the bean mixture and spoon over the mashed potatoes.

TUESDAY *Smoked Tofu à la King*

IMPERIAL/METRIC		AMERICAN
2 oz (55g)	mushrooms	1 cup
½ small	red pepper	½ small
6 oz (170g)	smoked tofu	¾ cup
2 tbs	vegan margarine	2 tbs
1 tbs	wholemeal (whole wheat) flour	1 tbs
¼ pint (140ml)	soya milk	⅔ cup
	sea salt and freshly ground black pepper to taste	
3 slices	wholemeal (whole wheat) toast	3 slices

1   Chop the mushrooms and red pepper. Dice the tofu. Heat half the margarine in a frying pan (skillet) and sauté these ingredients for a few minutes.
2   Meanwhile, heat the rest of the margarine in a saucepan and stir in the flour. Gradually pour in the milk, stirring constantly to avoid lumps. Bring to the boil, then simmer for 1–2 minutes to thicken. Season to taste.
3   Add the tofu mixture to the sauce and mix well. Cook for a further 1–2 minutes, then pile it onto the toast.

WEDNESDAY *Spaghetti with Bean and Caper Sauce*

IMPERIAL/METRIC		AMERICAN
3 oz (85g)	wholemeal (whole wheat) spaghetti	3 oz
1 small	onion	1 small
½ small	green pepper	½ small
1 small clove	garlic	1 small clove
1 tbs	olive oil	1 tbs
6	capers	6
1 tbs	tomato paste	1 tbs
3–4 fl oz (85–115ml)	water	⅓–½ cup
½ tsp	oregano	½ tsp
½ x 15½ oz (440g) can	borlotti (pinto) beans	½ x 15½ oz can
	freshly ground black pepper	

1. Cook the spaghetti in boiling salted water until just tender.
2. Chop the onion, green pepper and garlic finely. Heat the oil in a pan and sauté them for 3–4 minutes.
3. Chop the capers. Add them to the saucepan, along with the tomato paste, water and oregano. Bring to the boil, then lower the heat and simmer, uncovered, for about 5 minutes.
4. Drain and rinse the beans and add them to the pan with a little black pepper. Cook until the beans are thoroughly heated. Serve over the cooked drained spaghetti.

THURSDAY *Creamy Curried Mushrooms with Bulgur Wheat*

IMPERIAL/METRIC		AMERICAN
2½ oz (70g)	bulgur wheat	⅓ cup plus 1 tbs
8 fl oz (225ml)	water	1 cup
1 small	onion	1 small
1 tbs	vegan margarine	1 tbs
4 oz (115g)	mushrooms	2 cups
¼ tsp	coriander	¼ tsp
¼ tsp	cumin	¼ tsp
¼ tsp	turmeric	¼ tsp
¼ tsp	powdered ginger	¼ tsp
⅛ tsp	chilli powder	⅛ tsp
1 tbs	wholemeal (whole wheat) flour	1 tbs
½–⅔ cup	plain soya yogurt	½–⅔ cup
	sea salt to taste	
½ tsp	paprika	½ tsp

1 Put the bulgur wheat in a small saucepan, cover with the water (and a little sea salt) and bring to the boil. Then lower the heat, cover and simmer until the water is absorbed, which only takes about 10 minutes.

2 Chop the onion. Heat the margarine in a frying pan (skillet) and fry the onion until just beginning to brown. Slice the mushrooms and add them to the pan. Lower the heat and cook for about 3 minutes.

3 Grind the coriander and cumin if using whole seeds. Add the spices to the mushrooms and onions, and cook for 2–3 minutes longer, stirring occasionally.

4 In a small bowl, add the flour to the yogurt and stir well. Remove the mushroom mixture from the heat and stir in the yogurt mixture. Add salt to taste.

5 Spoon the bulgur wheat into a small fairly shallow ovenproof dish and spoon the mushroom mixture on top. Sprinkle with the paprika. Place under the grill (broiler) at medium heat and leave it there for about 5 minutes before transferring it onto a plate.

FRIDAY *Millet Pilaf*

IMPERIAL/METRIC		AMERICAN
1 small	onion	1 small
4 tsp	vegetable oil	4 tsp
2 oz (55g)	millet	¼ cup
	sea salt to taste	
¼ pint (140ml)	water	⅔ cup
2 oz (55g)	flaked (slivered) almonds	½ cup
1 small	leek	1 small
1 small	courgette (zucchini)	1 small
2 oz (55g)	mushrooms	1 cup
	freshly ground black pepper	
¼ tsp	ground cinnamon	¼ tsp

1　Chop the onion. Heat 2 tsp of the oil in a saucepan and sauté the onion for about 3 minutes until tender but not brown. Add the millet and cook for another 2 minutes or so, stirring occasionally. Sprinkle in the salt and pour in the water. Bring to the boil, then lower the heat and simmer, covered, for about 20 minutes.

2　Place the almonds under the grill (broiler) and toast until lightly browned, turning frequently. Set aside.

3　Chop the leek and courgette (zucchini) finely. Heat the remaining 2 tsp of oil in a frying pan (skillet) or wok and stir-fry the vegetables for about 3 minutes.

4　Slice the mushrooms thinly and add them to the leek and courgette (zucchini). Stir-fry for a further 2–3 minutes.

5　When the millet is tender and the water absorbed, stir in the vegetables, cinnamon and pepper to taste. Cook for a couple of minutes longer, stirring, then remove from the heat, and stir in the almonds.

SATURDAY LUNCH — *Green Bean Salad*

IMPERIAL/METRIC		AMERICAN
4 oz (115g)	green beans	¼ lb
1 small	onion	1 small
4 tsp	olive oil	4 tsp
½ small	green pepper	½ small
1 tsp	cider vinegar	1 tsp
	sea salt and freshly ground black pepper to taste	
1 oz (30g)	walnut pieces	3 tbs

1 Top and tail the beans and chop them into fairly small pieces. Steam them until crisp-tender.
2 Chop the onion finely. Heat 2 tsp of the oil in a frying pan (skillet) and fry the onion until lightly browned.
3 Chop the green pepper finely. In a bowl, combine the green pepper, beans and onion with the remaining 2 tsp of oil, the vinegar, and seasoning. Chill thoroughly.
4 Toast the walnut pieces under a grill (broiler) until lightly coloured. Cool. Just before eating the salad, mix the nuts into it. Accompany the salad with a slice of wholemeal (whole wheat) bread if desired.

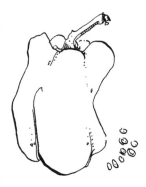

Week 2

Shopping list

VEGETABLES AND FRUIT

1 red pepper
1 small tomato
4 oz (115g) green beans
4 oz (115g) peas (about
 ½ lb (225g) before shelling)
3 small carrots
4 small onions
Garlic
Fresh ginger root
Fresh strawberries
10oz (285g) mung
 beansprouts
Chinese cabbage or spring
 cabbage (collards)
Lemon
1 small green pepper
4 oz (115g) mushrooms
Mixed salad ingredients
Spring onions (scallions)
¼ cucumber

MISCELLANEOUS

Flaked (slivered) almonds
10 oz (285g) tofu
Peanut butter
Wholemeal (whole wheat)
 or spinach noodles
Whole almonds
Sesame seeds
15½ oz (440g) can chick
 peas (garbanzo beans)
Tabasco sauce

Check that you have all the staples listed on pages xiii and xiv.

SUNDAY LUNCH   *Basque Salad*

IMPERIAL/METRIC		AMERICAN
1	red pepper	1
1 small	tomato	1 small
1½ tbs	olive oil	1½ tbs
2 tsp	cider vinegar	2 tsp
½ tsp	tomato paste	½ tsp
½ tsp	paprika	½ tsp
¼ tsp	garlic salt	¼ tsp
	freshly ground black pepper	
	2 or 3 slices wholemeal	
	(whole wheat) toast	

1 Cut the pepper into quarters, removing the seeds and pith while doing so.
2 Place the quarters, skin side facing upwards, under a hot grill (broiler) until
   the skin is blistered and blackened; move the quarters around once or twice
   if necessary to ensure evenness.
3 Cool slightly, then place the quarters under cold running water, and peel off
   the skins. Slice them into thin strips and chill.
4 Scald, skin, and slice the tomato thinly.
5 In a small bowl mix together the oil, vinegar, tomato paste, paprika, garlic salt,
   and pepper.
6 At lunchtime place the pepper strips and tomato slices on top of the toast,
   and spoon the dressing over everything.

Vegetable Pilau Special

IMPERIAL/METRIC		AMERICAN
3 oz (85g)	long-grain brown rice	½ cup
	sea salt to taste	
1 tsp	turmeric	1 tsp
2 oz (55g)	fresh green beans	2 oz
1 small	carrot	1 small
2 oz (55g) (about 4 oz/115g before shelling)	shelled peas	⅓ cup
1 small	onion	1 small
1 small clove	garlic	1 small clove
¼–½ inch piece	fresh ginger root	¼–½ inch piece
1 small	tomato	1 small
1 tbs	vegan margarine	1 tbs
1 tsp	ground coriander	1 tsp
1 tsp	ground cumin	1 tsp
¼ tsp	chilli powder (optional)	¼ tsp
1 tsp	garam masala	1 tsp
1 oz (30g)	flaked (slivered) almonds	¼ cup

1 Cover the rice with boiling water and leave to soak for several hours. Drain, rinse, cover with water, add a little salt and the turmeric; bring to the boil, then lower the heat, and cook for about 20 minutes until the water is absorbed and the rice tender.
2 Meanwhile, chop the beans and carrot. Steam them – and the peas – until just tender. Drain and set aside.
3 Chop the onion and the tomato. Crush the garlic. Grate the ginger finely.
4 Heat the margarine in a pan and add the onion. Sauté until beginning to brown. Add the garlic and ginger and cook for a minute longer. Lower the heat and stir in the spices. Then add the tomato and cook for a minute or two longer. Remove from the heat and stir in the cooked vegetables.
5 Place half the cooked rice on the bottom of a greased ovenproof dish, spoon the vegetable mixture over it, then top with the other half of the rice. Cover the dish (if it has no lid then use foil) and bake it at 350°F (180°C) Gas Mark 4 for about half an hour. Alternatively, cover with greaseproof paper and microwave for 2 minutes.
6 Toast the almonds under a hot grill (broiler) until lightly browned. When the pilau is ready and dished up, sprinkle the almonds on top.

SUNDAY DESSERT — Strawberry 'Cheese'

IMPERIAL/METRIC

1 x 5 oz (150g) carton	natural (plain) soya yogurt	1 x 5 oz carton
	a few fresh strawberries	
	raw cane sugar to taste	

AMERICAN

1 Spoon the yogurt carefully into a square of muslin or cheesecloth. Gather it up and tie it round the taps of the sink (or somewhere else convenient over a bowl) and leave it to drip for several hours or overnight. Spoon the result – which will be about 1½ oz (45g) in weight and resemble *fromage frais* in texture – into a small bowl and refrigerate until ready to use.

2 Mash the strawberries coarsely in a small bowl. Stir in the yogurt 'cheese' and sugar to taste.

MONDAY *Peanut Buttery Stir-fry*

IMPERIAL/METRIC		AMERICAN
2½–3 oz (70–85g)	brown rice*	½ cup
3 oz (85g)	tofu	⅓ cup
4 tsp	vegetable oil	4 tsp
1 small	onion	1 small
1 small	carrot	1 small
2 oz (55g)	green beans	2 oz
	a few leaves of Chinese or spring cabbage (collards)	
3 oz (85g)	mung beansprouts	1½ cups
1 small clove	garlic	1 small clove
¼-inch piece	fresh ginger root	¼-inch piece
1½ tbs	peanut butter	1½ tbs
4 tbs	water	4 tbs
2 tsp	lemon juice	2 tsp
1 tbs	soya sauce	1 tbs
2 tbs	soya milk	2 tbs

* If making the whole week's menus, cook double the amount of rice, cool and then refrigerate half of it.

1 Cook the rice until tender.
2 Dice the tofu. Heat 1 tsp of the oil in a wok or frying pan (skillet) and stir-fry the tofu until lightly browned. Remove from the wok.
3 Slice the onion thinly. Slice the carrot into matchsticks. Chop the beans finely. Heat 2 tsp of the oil in the wok and stir-fry these ingredients for 2–3 minutes.
4 Chop the cabbage leaves and add them to the wok along with the beansprouts. Continue stir-frying until just tender.
5 Crush the garlic. Grate the ginger finely. Heat the remaining tsp of oil in a small saucepan and add the garlic and ginger. Cook for a minute or two, then stir in the peanut butter and then the water. Stir until smooth. (This much can be done before the vegetables start cooking; the rest should wait until they are nearly ready.) Add the lemon juice, soya sauce and milk, and stir well.
6 Return the tofu to the wok, and stir in the peanut butter sauce. Mix well and serve on top of the rice.

TUESDAY *Mediterranean Noodles*

IMPERIAL/METRIC		AMERICAN
1 small	onion	1 small
½ small	green pepper	½ small
1 small clove	garlic	1 small clove
1 tbs	olive oil	1 tbs
2 oz (55g)	mushrooms	1 cup
3 fl oz (90ml)	vegetable stock or water	⅓ cup
2 tbs	tomato paste	2 tbs
1 tsp	oregano	1 tsp
	sea salt and freshly ground black pepper to taste	
3–3½ oz (85–100g)	wholemeal (whole wheat) or spinach noodles	3–3½ oz
1 tsp	vegan margarine	1 tsp
1 tbs	nutritional yeast flakes (powder) or	1 tbs
1 tsp	vegan Parmesan	1 tsp

1 Chop the onion and green pepper finely. Crush the garlic. Heat the oil in a pan and sauté these ingredients for 3–4 minutes.
2 Slice the mushrooms and add them to the pan. Cook for about 2 minutes longer.
3 Add the stock or water, tomato paste, oregano and seasoning. Bring to the boil, then lower the heat and leave to simmer, uncovered, for about 10 minutes.
4 Meanwhile, cook the noodles until just tender. Drain them and toss them with the margarine and yeast or vegan Parmesan. Transfer them to a plate and pour the sauce on top.

WEDNESDAY *Vegetable Fried Rice*

IMPERIAL/METRIC		AMERICAN
2½–3 oz (70–85g)	brown rice	½ cup
½ oz (15g)	almonds	⅛ cup
1 tbs	sesame seeds	1 tbs
1 small	onion	1 small
1 small	carrot	1 small
1 tbs	vegetable oil	1 tbs
3–4 oz (85–115g)	Chinese or spring cabbage (collards)	3–4 oz
2 oz (55g)	shelled peas	⅓ cup
(about 4 oz/115g		
before shelling)		
4 oz (115g)	mung beansprouts	2 cups
3 oz (85g)	tofu	⅓ cup
1 tbs	soya sauce	1 tbs
	freshly ground black pepper	

1 Cook the rice until tender or use rice cooked earlier in the week.
2 Toast the almonds and sesame seeds lightly under the grill (broiler). Set aside.
3 Chop the onion and carrot finely. Heat the oil in a wok or frying pan (skillet) and stir-fry the onion and carrot for about 2 minutes.
4 Shred the cabbage. Add it to the wok, along with the peas and beansprouts. Cover the wok and cook for about 3 minutes, uncovering it to stir it once, by which time the cabbage should have wilted.
5 Mash the tofu in a small bowl. Add it to the wok along with the rice. Mix well. Season with soya sauce and pepper to taste. Stir-fry the whole mixture until thoroughly heated.
6 Remove from the heat and stir in the toasted almonds and sesame seeds.

THURSDAY *Chick Pea (Garbanzo Bean) Burgers*

IMPERIAL/METRIC		AMERICAN
½ can	chick peas (garbanzo beans)	½ can
1	spring onion (scallion)	1
1 tbs	soya yogurt	1 tbs
1 tsp	tomato paste	1 tsp
1 tsp	soya sauce	1 tsp
½ tsp	marjoram	½ tsp
1 oz (30g)	wholemeal (whole wheat) breadcrumbs	½ cup
as required	wholemeal (whole wheat) flour	as required
as required	vegetable oil	as required
	mixed salad ingredients	

1 Drain and rinse the chick peas (garbanzo beans). Mash them in a bowl.
2 Chop the spring onion (scallion) finely. Add it to the bowl, along with the yogurt, tomato paste, soya sauce, marjoram and breadcrumbs. Mix well, and form into 3 burgers.
3 Spread a little flour on a plate. Turn the burgers in the flour so that they are coated on each side. Refrigerate them for about half an hour (or longer if more convenient).
4 Shallow fry the burgers in a little oil until browned on both sides. Serve with a mixed side salad.

FRIDAY *Spaghetti Stir-fry*

IMPERIAL/METRIC		AMERICAN
3 oz (85g)	wholemeal (whole wheat) spaghetti	3 oz
1–2	spring onions (scallions)	1–2
1 small clove	garlic	1 small clove
½-inch piece	fresh ginger root	½-inch piece
4 tbs	vegetable oil	4 tbs
4 oz (115g)	tofu	½ cup
½ small	green pepper	½ small
2 oz (55g)	mushrooms	1 cup
3–4 oz (85–115g)	fresh mung beansprouts	3–4 oz
1 tbs	soya sauce	1 tbs
½-inch piece	cucumber	½-inch piece

1 Cook the spaghetti until tender.
2 Chop the spring onion (scallion), garlic and ginger very finely. Heat
   2 tbs of the oil in a wok or frying pan (skillet), and stir-fry these ingredients for
   about 2 minutes. Dice the tofu and add it to the wok; stir-fry for another
   minute. Remove the tofu mixture from the wok.
3 Chop the green pepper and mushrooms. Heat the remaining 2 tbs of oil in
   the wok and stir-fry these ingredients for 1 minute. Add the beansprouts and
   stir-fry for another minute.
4 Return the tofu mixture to the wok, and add the cooked spaghetti as well.
   Sprinkle in the soya sauce, mix it all very well and stir-fry the whole thing for
   another minute.
5 Chop the cucumber very finely and sprinkle it over the top.

SATURDAY LUNCH *Piquant Chick Pea (Garbanzo Bean) Spread*

IMPERIAL/METRIC		AMERICAN
½ x 15 oz (440g) can	chick peas (garbanzo beans)	½ x 15 oz can
1 tbs	soya yogurt	1 tbs
½ tsp	ground cumin	½ tsp
½ tsp	ground coriander	½ tsp
	few drops Tabasco sauce	

1 Drain and rinse the chick peas (garbanzo beans). Put them in a bowl and mash them coarsely. Stir in the yogurt, cumin, coriander and Tabasco sauce.
2 Serve in sandwiches or rolls, with lettuce or alfalfa sprouts if desired.

Week 3

Shopping list

VEGETABLES AND FRUIT
Spring onions (scallions)
1 lb (455g) potatoes (plus
 1 extra)
Olives
½ lb (225g) mushrooms
Lemon
Mixed salad ingredients
¼ lb (115g) gooseberries
1 small onion
½ lb (225g) courgettes
 (zucchini) (plus 1 extra)
½ lb (225g) (¼ lb/115g
 shelled) peas
1 small leek
1 small red pepper
1 small green pepper
Garlic
Fresh ginger root
4–6 oz (115–170g) tomatoes

MISCELLANEOUS
Rolled oats
10 oz (285g) packet tofu
Miso
Tahini
7 oz (200g) can butter (lima)
 beans

Check that you have all the staples listed on pages xiii and xiv.

Mediterranean-style Potato Salad with Yogurt Dressing

IMPERIAL/METRIC		AMERICAN
½ lb (225g)	potatoes*	½ lb
¼ pint (140ml)	soya yogurt	⅔ cup
1	spring onion (scallion)	1
3	olives	3
¼–½ tsp	garlic salt	¼–½ tsp
½ tsp	oregano	½ tsp
1 tbs	olive oil	1 tbs

1　Cook the potatoes until tender. Cool slightly.
2　Put the yogurt in a bowl. Chop the spring onion (scallion) and olives finely and add them to the bowl along with the garlic salt, oregano and olive oil. Mix well.
3　Dice the potatoes and add them to the bowl. Mix them in. Cover bowl and chill thoroughly. (This is fairly substantial on its own, but crispbread, toast or toasted pitta bread provide a pleasantly contrasting texture.)

* If making the entire week's menus then cook 1 lb (455g) potatoes; cool half of them and then refrigerate for use later in the week.

SUNDAY DINNER Savoury Mushroom Bake

IMPERIAL/METRIC		AMERICAN
1 oz (30g)	wholemeal (whole wheat) flour	¼ cup
1 oz (30g)	rolled oats	¼ cup
¼–½ tsp	garlic salt	¼–½ tsp
1 oz (30g)	vegan margarine	¼ cup
4 oz (115g)	mushrooms	2 cups
2 tsp	vegetable oil	2 tsp
3 oz (85g)	tofu*	⅓ cup
1 tbs	soya yogurt*	1 tbs
1 tbs	water*	1 tbs
½ tsp	miso*	½ tsp
1 tsp	tahini*	1 tsp
1 tsp	lemon juice*	1 tsp
1 tsp	paprika*	1 tsp
	mixed salad ingredients	

1 Mix the flour, oats and garlic salt in a bowl. Rub in the margarine finely. Put the mixture in a greased ovenproof dish and bake at 375°F (190°C) Gas Mark 5 for about 10 minutes.
2 Slice the mushrooms. Sauté them in the oil for 3–4 minutes.
3 Put the tofu, yogurt, water, miso, tahini, lemon juice and paprika into a liquidizer and blend thoroughly.
4 Stir the sautéed mushrooms into the tofu mixture. Spoon this on top of the flour and oat base, return to the oven and bake for 20–25 minutes. Serve the dish with a mixed salad.

• If making the whole week's menus then double the amount of each of these ingredients; spoon half of the mixture into an airtight container and refrigerate for use later in the week. Halve the remainder of the tofu (4–5 oz/115–140g) from the shopping list and put it in the freezer for Friday's recipe (page 32).

SUNDAY DESSERT — *Gooseberry Dessert*

IMPERIAL/METRIC		AMERICAN
4 oz (115g)	gooseberries	¼ lb
¼ pint (140ml)	water	⅔ cup
	raw cane sugar to taste	
½ oz (15g)	semolina (farina)	⅛ cup

1 Top and tail the gooseberries and place them in a saucepan. Cover them with the water and sugar. Bring to the boil, then lower the heat, cover, and simmer until the gooseberries are tender.
2 Stir in the semolina (farina) carefully, and simmer for a couple of minutes longer until the mixture thickens.
3 Cool, then chill thoroughly.

MONDAY *Macaroni Stew*

IMPERIAL/METRIC		AMERICAN
3 oz (85g)	wholemeal (whole wheat) macaroni (or other pasta shape)*	3 oz
1 small	onion	1 small
1 tbs	vegetable oil	1 tbs
1 small	courgette (zucchini)	1 small
1 small	potato	1 small
2 oz (55g)	shelled fresh peas	⅓ cup
¼ pint (140ml)	water	⅔ cup
1 tsp	yeast extract	1 tsp
1	bay leaf	1

1 Cook the pasta until tender.
2 Chop the onion. Sauté it in the oil in a saucepan for 2–3 minutes.
3 Chop the courgette (zucchini) into thick slices. Dice the potato finely. Add these ingredients to the onion. Sauté for another minute or two, stirring.
4 Add the peas, water, yeast extract and bay leaf. Bring to the boil, then lower the heat, cover the pan, and simmer for 7–10 minutes.
5 Add the cooked drained pasta to the vegetables and cook for a minute or two longer. Remove the bay leaf before dishing up. (NB. This dish is easier to eat with a spoon than a fork.)

* If making the whole week's menus then cook double this amount of pasta. Cool half of it, then rinse it (to avoid stickiness), drain and refrigerate it in an airtight container for use later in the week.

TUESDAY *Butter (Lima) Bean and Vegetable Stew*

IMPERIAL/METRIC		AMERICAN
2½–3 oz (70–85g)	brown rice*	½ cup
1 small	leek	1 small
1 tbs	vegetable oil	1 tbs
2 oz (55g)	mushrooms	1 cup
½ small	red pepper	½ small
1	bay leaf	1
¼ pint (140ml)	water or vegetable stock	⅔ cup
1 x 7 oz (200g) can	butter (lima) beans	1 x 7 oz can
1 tbs	peanut butter	1 tbs
	soya sauce to taste	

1 Cook the rice until tender.
2 Clean the leek well and chop it finely. Sauté in the oil for 2–3 minutes.
3 Slice the mushrooms. Chop the red pepper finely. Add them to the pan and sauté for a further 2 minutes. Add the bay leaf and the water or stock; bring to the boil, then lower the heat, cover the pan and simmer for 5–7 minutes.
4 Drain and rinse the beans.
5 Add the peanut butter to the vegetables in the pan and mix well. Add the beans, taste for seasoning, and add soya sauce. Continue simmering gently until the beans are thoroughly heated; remove bay leaf and serve over the rice.

* If making the whole week's menus then cook double this amount of rice; cool and then refrigerate half.

WEDNESDAY *Macaroni au Gratin*

IMPERIAL/METRIC		AMERICAN
	Tofu mixture from Sunday Dinner	
2 tbs	water	2 tbs
2 tsp	tomato paste	2 tsp
2 tbs	nutritional yeast flakes or powder or	2 tbs
2 tsp	vegan Parmesan	2 tsp
3 oz (85g)	macaroni (or other pasta shape), cooked	3 oz
1 oz (30g)	wholemeal (whole wheat) breadcrumbs	½ cup
1–2 tsp	vegan margarine	1–2 tsp
	mixed salad ingredients	

1 If you do not have the tofu mixture already prepared then turn to page 26 for the recipe. Turn the mixture into a bowl; add the water, tomato paste and 1 tbs of the yeast or 1 tsp of the vegan Parmesan and stir.
2 Add the cooked macaroni to the bowl and mix thoroughly. Turn the mixture into a greased oven dish; top with the breadcrumbs, the remaining yeast or Parmesan, and the margarine. Bake at 350°F (180°C) Gas Mark 4 for about half an hour. Accompany with a mixed green salad.

THURSDAY *Indian Rice*

IMPERIAL/METRIC		AMERICAN
1 small	onion	1 small
1 small clove	garlic	1 small clove
¼-inch piece	fresh ginger root	¼-inch piece
1 tbs	vegetable oil	1 tbs
½ tsp	ground cumin	½ tsp
¼ tsp	ground coriander	¼ tsp
½ tsp	turmeric	½ tsp
½ tsp	garam masala	½ tsp
pinch	chilli powder	pinch
4–6 oz (115–170g)	tomatoes	¼ lb
1 small	carrot	1 small
½ small	red pepper	½ small
2 oz (55g) (about 4 oz/115g unshelled)	shelled peas	⅓ cup
2 tbs	water	2 tbs
2½–3 oz (70–85g)	brown rice, cooked	½ cup
	sea salt to taste	

1 Chop the onion, garlic and ginger finely. Heat the oil in a pan and sauté the onion, garlic and ginger for 2–3 minutes.
2 Add the spices to the pan and stir briefly.
3 Chop the tomatoes, carrot and red pepper. Add them to the saucepan along with the peas. Stir well for a minute or two. Add the water, bring to the boil then lower the heat, cover the pan and leave to simmer for about 5 minutes.
4 Stir in the cooked rice and add salt to taste. Continue cooking in the covered pan for about 5 minutes longer, stirring once or twice, before dishing up.

Friday Tofu and Green Pepper Savoury

IMPERIAL/METRIC		AMERICAN
1 tbs	yeast extract	1 tbs
¼ pint (140ml)	boiling water	⅔ cup
4–5 oz (115–140g)	frozen tofu	½–⅔ cup
1	spring onion (scallion)	1
1 small clove	garlic	1 small clove
1 small	green pepper	1 small
2 oz (55g)	mushrooms	1 cup
2 tbs	vegetable oil	2 tbs
½ lb (225g)	potatoes, cooked	½ lb
1 tbs	cornflour (cornstarch)	1 tbs
1 tbs	cold water	1 tbs
	sea salt and freshly ground black pepper to taste	

1 Dissolve the yeast extract in the boiling water in a bowl and add the frozen tofu pieces. Cover and leave for 10 minutes until the tofu has defrosted. (If at that time the tofu still has a hard centre and the liquid has cooled off, the mixture can be refreshed with more boiling water and yeast extract.)

2 Chop the spring onion (scallion) and garlic finely. Cut the green pepper into thin strips. Slice the mushrooms.

3 When the tofu has defrosted, squeeze gently and slice. Keep the soaking liquid.

4 Heat 1 tbs of the oil in a saucepan and add the tofu. Fry the slices for a minute, then turn them over and fry the other side for a minute. Add the spring onion (scallion), garlic, green pepper and mushrooms. Pour in 2½–3 fl oz (75–90ml)/½ cup of the yeast extract liquid. Bring to the boil, then lower the heat, cover the pan and simmer for about 10 minutes.

5 Slice the cooked potatoes. Heat the remaining tbs of oil in a frying pan and sauté the potatoes until lightly browned on both sides. Season to taste.

6 Mix the cornflour (cornstarch) and water and stir into the tofu mixture. Simmer for a minute or two until thickened, then dish up with the potatoes.

SATURDAY LUNCH *Mediterranean-style Courgette (Zucchini) Salad*

IMPERIAL/METRIC		AMERICAN
½ lb (225g)	courgettes (zucchini)	½ lb
1 tbs	olive oil	1 tbs
1 tsp	lemon juice	1 tsp
¼ tsp	garlic salt	¼ tsp
	freshly ground black pepper	
1 tsp	dried mint or	1 tsp
1 tbs	finely chopped fresh mint	1 tbs

1 Halve the courgettes (zucchini) across their width, then slice into thick matchsticks. Cook them in just enough water to cover the bottom of the pan for 2–3 minutes and drain.
2 In a bowl combine the oil, lemon juice, garlic salt, pepper to taste and mint. Add the courgettes (zucchini) while still warm and mix well. Chill thoroughly. (Nice with thick slabs of wholemeal/whole wheat bread.)

Week 4

Shopping list

VEGETABLES AND FRUIT
½ lb (225g) new potatoes
Spring onions (scallions)
2 small courgettes (zucchini)
5 small onions
1 small tomato
¼ lb (115g) rhubarb
½ lb (225g) green beans
Garlic
Lemon
Celery
1 small leek
Parsley
¼ lb (115g) mushrooms
2 oz (55g) broad (fava) beans
   (about 6 oz (170g) before
   shelling)
Salad ingredients

MISCELLANEOUS
15½ oz (440g) can haricot
   (navy) beans
Vegan mayonnaise
9–10 oz (255–285g) tofu
Dates
Creamed coconut
1 oz (30g) roasted cashews
1 oz (30g) pine (pignolia)
   nuts

Check that you have all the staples listed on pages xiii and xiv.

SUNDAY LUNCH — *Bean and Potato Salad*

IMPERIAL/METRIC		AMERICAN
½ lb (225g)	new potatoes	½ lb
1–2	spring onions (scallions)	1–2
½ x 15½ oz (440g) can	haricot (navy) beans	½ x 15½ oz can
1 tbs	vegan mayonnaise	1 tbs
⅛ pint (70ml)	soya yogurt	⅓ cup
	black pepper to taste	

1 Scrub the potatoes and cook them in lightly salted water until tender. Drain them and when they are cool enough to handle dice them.
2 Chop the spring onions (scallions) finely. Put them in a bowl with the potatoes. Add the beans (drained), mayonnaise, yogurt and seasoning. Mix well, then chill thoroughly. (As an accompaniment, crispbread provides a particularly nice contrast in texture.)

SUNDAY DINNER Courgette (Zucchini) and Tomato Flan

IMPERIAL/METRIC		AMERICAN
1½ oz (45g)	wholemeal (whole wheat) flour*	⅓ cup
¾ oz (15g)	vegan margarine*	⅙ cup
pinch	sea salt	pinch
1 small	onion	1 small
1 tbs	vegetable oil	1 tbs
1 small	courgette (zucchini)	1 small
4 oz (115g)	tofu	½ cup
3 oz (85g)	nutritional yeast flakes or powder	1 tbs
½ tsp	basil (sweet)	½ tsp
	sea salt and freshly ground black pepper to taste	
1 small	tomato	1 small

1 Combine the flour, margarine and salt and add enough water to make pastry. Roll out and place in a small greased flan tin.
2 Chop the onion and sauté it for about 5 minutes in the oil. Slice the courgette (zucchini) and add it to the pan, continue to cook for 3–4 minutes longer.
3 Prick the pastry with a fork and bake it for about 5 minutes at 400°F (200°C) Gas Mark 6.
4 Mash the tofu. Mix with the yeast, basil and seasoning, then stir into the vegetables.
5 Skin and slice the tomato. Stir it into the mixture. Turn this into the flan case. Lower the oven temperature to 375°F (190°C) Gas Mark 5 and bake for about half an hour. Accompany the flan with a side salad.

*If making the whole week's menus then use 4 oz (115g)/1 cup flour and 2 oz (55g)/¼ cup margarine to make the pastry. Use just over one third of it for this recipe; wrap the remainder in clingfilm and refrigerate.

SUNDAY DESSERT Rhubarb and Date Cream

IMPERIAL/METRIC		AMERICAN
4 oz (115g)	rhubarb	¼ lb
2 oz (55g)	dates	⅓ cup
4 tbs	water	4 tbs
1 oz (30g)	creamed coconut	1 oz

1 Chop the rhubarb and dates. Cook them with the water at a low heat for 10–15 minutes.
2 Grate or chop the creamed coconut and add it to the saucepan. Beat well. Spoon the mixture into a dessert bowl; cool, then chill.

MONDAY *Cashew and Vegetable Curry*

IMPERIAL/METRIC		AMERICAN
2½–3 oz (65–85g)	brown rice*	½ cup
1 small	carrot	1 small
1 small	courgette (zucchini)	1 small
2 oz (55g)	green beans	2 oz
4 tbs	water	4 tbs
1 small	onion	1 small
1 small clove	garlic	1 small clove
1 tbs	vegetable oil	1 tbs
½ tsp	ground coriander	½ tsp
½ tsp	ground cumin	½ tsp
½ tsp	turmeric	½ tsp
¼ tsp	powdered ginger	¼ tsp
⅛ tsp	chilli powder	⅛ tsp
1 tbs	tomato paste	1 tbs
1 tsp	lemon juice	1 tsp
2 tbs	soya yogurt	2 tbs
1 oz (30g)	roasted cashew nuts**	¼ cup

* If making the whole week's menus then cook double this quantity, cool and then refrigerate half of it for use on Friday.
** If buying the salted kind then it's a good idea to wash the salt off before using. Raw ones can be roasted under the grill (broiler).

1   Cook the rice until tender.
2   Chop the carrot, courgette (zucchini) and beans and cook them in the water
    until just tender.
3   Chop the onion; crush the garlic. Sauté them in the oil in a saucepan for
    3–4 minutes. Stir in all the spices and cook over a very low heat for another
    minute. Stir in the tomato paste and lemon juice.
4   Add the vegetables to the pan, along with their cooking liquid. Cook,
    uncovered, for another minute or two.
5   Stir in the yogurt and heat gently without boiling. Add the cashews and pour
    over the cooked rice. (This is nice with chutney.)

TUESDAY *Tofu and Vegetable Stew*

IMPERIAL/METRIC		AMERICAN
2 oz (55g)	green beans*	2 oz
1 small	carrot*	1 small
1 stick	celery*	1 stick
1 small	onion*	1 small
1 tbs	vegetable oil*	1 tbs
3–4 oz (85–115g)	tofu*	⅓–½ cup
1 tbs	wholemeal (whole wheat) flour*	1 tbs
1 tbs	soya sauce*	1 tbs
½ tsp	sage*	½ tsp
	sea salt and freshly ground	
	black pepper to taste	
	wholemeal (whole wheat) bread,	
	rice or bulgur wheat to serve (optional)	

1 Chop the beans, carrot and celery. Cover with boiling water and cook until crisp-tender. Drain, retaining the stock.

2 Chop the onion. Sauté in the oil for about 3 minutes. Dice the tofu and add it to the pan. Sauté for a few minutes longer, stirring frequently. Sprinkle in the flour and stir. Gradually add ⅛ pint (70ml)/⅔ cup vegetable stock.* Stir until thickened.

3 Add the soya sauce, sage, seasoning and the cooked vegetables to the pan. Stir well and simmer, uncovered, for 3–4 minutes longer. Accompany with wedges of bread or serve over cooked rice or bulgur wheat.

* If making the whole week's dishes then double all of these ingredients and refrigerate half the stew for use on Thursday.

WEDNESDAY Bulgur, Bean and Celery Casserole

IMPERIAL/METRIC		AMERICAN
2½ oz (70g)	bulgur wheat	½ cup
1 small	onion	1 small
1 tbs	vegetable oil	1 tbs
1 small clove	garlic	1 small clove
2 oz (55g)	mushrooms	1 cup
2 sticks	celery	2 sticks
1 tsp	rosemary	1 tsp
½ x 15½ oz (440g) can	haricot (navy) beans	½ x 15½ oz can
1 tsp	lemon juice	1 tsp
	freshly ground black pepper	

1 Cook the bulgur wheat with about three times its volume of water (the exact amount never seems to make much difference) and a little sea salt. (This should only take a few minutes.)

2 Chop the onion. Sauté it in the oil in a largish saucepan for 2–3 minutes. Crush the garlic and add it to the pan; cook for a minute or two longer.

3 Slice the mushrooms. Chop the celery. Add them to the pan along with the rosemary (N.B. dried rosemary is best ground with a pestle and mortar before use). Stir well, cover the pan, lower the heat and leave to cook for a few minutes.

4 Drain and rinse the beans. Add them to the pan along with the lemon juice and pepper to taste. Stir well and heat for a couple of minutes, then stir in the cooked bulgur wheat. Mix and cook for a couple of minutes more; taste for seasoning before dishing up.

T~~hurs~~day *Tofu Pot Pie*

IMPERIAL/METRIC		AMERICAN
2½ oz (70g)	Pastry made from wholemeal	½ cup
	(whole wheat) flour and	
1¼ oz (35g)	vegan margarine or	¼ cup
	the remaining pastry from Sunday's flan	
	(page 36)	
	Tofu stew (see page 40)	

1 Roll out about two-thirds of the pastry on a floured board and put it into a small oiled deep pie dish. Prick the pastry and bake it at 450°F (230°C) Gas Mark 8 for about 5 minutes.
2 Meanwhile, roll out the rest of the pastry. Remove the pie dish from the oven and reduce the oven temperature to 400°F (200°C) Gas Mark 6. Spoon the tofu stew mixture into the pastry and top with the remainder of the pastry. Prick with a fork and bake for about 25 minutes.

FRIDAY *Mediterranean-style Fried Rice*

IMPERIAL/METRIC		AMERICAN
1 oz (30g)	pine (pignolia) nuts*	2 tbs
1 small	onion	1 small
1 small	leek	1 small
1 tbs	olive oil	1 tbs
2½–3 oz (70–85g)	brown rice, cooked	½ cup
juice and grated rind of ½ small	lemon	juice and grated rind of ½ small
2 tsp	tomato paste	2 tsp
	sea salt and freshly ground black pepper to taste	
2 tsp	chopped parsley	2 tsp

1 Toast the nuts lightly under the grill (broiler). Set aside.
2 Chop the onion and cleaned leek. Sauté them in the oil for 2–3 minutes.
3 Add the rice, lemon juice and rind, tomato paste and seasoning. Stir well. Cook the mixture over a fairly low heat for 7–10 minutes, stirring frequently.
4 Stir in the parsley and toasted nuts and dish up immediately.

---

* These are undeniably very expensive, but they are so rich that a small amount of them goes a long way, and their flavour is unique.

SATURDAY LUNCH Bean and Mushroom Salad

IMPERIAL/METRIC		AMERICAN
2 oz (55g)	green beans	2 oz
2 oz (55g)	shelled broad (fava) beans	2 oz
(about 6 oz (170g) before shelling)		
2 oz (55g)	button mushrooms	2 oz
1½ tbs	vegan mayonnaise	1½ tbs
1 tbs	soya yogurt	1 tbs
	sea salt and freshly ground black pepper to taste	

1　Top and tail the green beans and slice them into bite-sized pieces. Cook until crisp-tender and drain.
2　Cook the shelled broad (fava) beans until tender and drain.
3　Clean and slice the mushrooms.
4　Put all of the beans and the mushrooms into a bowl; add the mayonnaise and yogurt, stir well and season to taste. Chill.

Week 5

Shopping list

VEGETABLES AND FRUIT

Spring onions (scallions)
Parsley
Mixed salad ingredients
6 small onions
6–8 oz (170–225g) seasonal
  green vegetables
6 oz (170g) plums
2 small courgettes (zucchini)
4 small tomatoes
Garlic
¼ cucumber*
1 small carrot
2 oz (55g) mushrooms

MISCELLANEOUS

4 oz (115g) mixed nuts
9–10 oz (255–285g) tofu
1 x 15½ oz (440g) can chick
  peas (garbanzo beans)
Mango chutney
Smokey Snaps (imitation
  bacon bits)
3 oz (85g) red lentils
7 oz (200g) can tomatoes

Check that you have all the staples listed on pages xiii and xiv.

* ⅛ for recipe; use the rest as part of the mixed salad ingredients.

SUNDAY LUNCH *Nut Balls and Salad*

IMPERIAL/METRIC		AMERICAN
2 oz (55g)	mixed nuts	½ cup
1 oz (30g)	wholemeal (whole wheat) breadcrumbs	½ cup
1 tsp	olive oil	1 tsp
2 tsp	tomato paste	2 tsp
1	spring onion (scallion)	1
1 tbs	parsley	1 tbs
	mixed salad ingredients	

1 Grind the nuts. In a bowl mix the nuts and breadcrumbs, and add the oil and tomato paste.

2 Chop the spring onion (scallion) and parsley finely and add them to the bowl. Mix well, then knead into walnut-sized balls. Refrigerate, then serve on top of a mixed salad.

SUNDAY DINNER *Scalloped Tofu au Gratin*

IMPERIAL/METRIC		AMERICAN
¾ oz (20g)	hard vegan margarine (e.g. Tomor)*	1½ tbs
1 oz (30g)	soya flour*	¼ cup
½–¾ tsp	yeast extract*	½–¾ tsp
1 small	onion	1 small
2 tbs	vegetable oil	2 tbs
5–6 oz (140–170g)	firm tofu	¾ cup
1 tbs	wholemeal (whole wheat) flour	1 tbs
4 fl oz (115ml)	soya milk	½ cup
	sea salt and freshly ground black pepper to taste	
1½ oz (45g)	wholemeal (whole wheat) breadcrumbs	¾ cup
1 tbs	nutritional yeast flakes or powder	1 tbs
6–8 oz (170–225g)	seasonal green vegetable	6–8 oz

* If making the whole week's menus then double these ingredients; follow the instructions under 1 above; when chilled cut in half and keep half of it in the refrigerator until required.

1 Melt the margarine in a small saucepan over a low heat. Remove from the heat and stir in the soya flour and yeast extract. Pour the mixture onto an oiled flat tin or plate; cool then chill until ready to use.

2 Chop the onion finely and sauté it in half the oil in a frying pan (skillet) for 2–3 minutes. Dice the tofu and add it to the frying pan (skillet). Sauté for a further 2–3 minutes, stirring frequently. Remove from the heat.

3 In a small saucepan heat the remaining tbs of oil and stir in the flour. Gradually add the milk, stirring constantly to avoid lumps. When boiling and thickened add seasoning. Remove from the heat.

4 Dice the soya flour mixture finely. Add half to the white sauce and stir well. Season to taste, then stir in the tofu and onion.

5 Turn the mixture into an oiled baking dish. Mix the breadcrumbs with the dry yeast and sprinkle on the top along with the remainder of the diced soya flour mixture.

6 Bake at 350°F (180°C) Gas Mark 4 for 20–30 minutes, until lightly browned on top. Accompany with a lightly-steamed seasonal green vegetable.

SUNDAY DESSERT *Nutty Plum Crumble*

IMPERIAL/METRIC		AMERICAN
1 oz (30g)	wholemeal (whole wheat) flour	¼ cup
¼ oz (20g)	rolled oats	⅙ cup
	raw cane sugar to taste	
½ oz (15g)	vegan margarine	1 tbs
½ oz (15g)	peanut butter	1 tbs
6 oz (170g)	plums	6 oz
1 tbs	water	1 tbs

1 Put the flour, oats and sugar in a bowl. Rub in the margarine and peanut butter finely.
2 Slice the plums. Put them in a baking dish with the water. Cover with the crumble mixture. Bake at 375°F (180°C) Gas Mark 5 for about half an hour until lightly browned on top.

MONDAY *Greek-style Courgette (Zucchini) and Chick Pea (Garbanzo Bean) Stew*

IMPERIAL/METRIC		AMERICAN
2½–3 oz (70–85g)	brown rice*	½ cup
1 small	onion	1 small
1 tbs	olive oil	1 tbs
1 small	courgette (zucchini)	1 small
2 small	tomatoes	2 small
2 tsp	tomato paste	2 tsp
½ tsp	marjoram	½ tsp
	sea salt and freshly ground black pepper to taste	
½ x 15½ oz (440g) can	chick peas (garbanzo beans)	½ x 15½ oz can
⅛ pint (70ml)	water	⅓ cup

1 Cook the rice until tender.
2 Slice the onion thinly. Sauté it in the oil in a saucepan for 2–3 minutes. Slice the courgette (zucchini) thinly and add it to the pan. Sauté for a further 4–5 minutes.
3 Skin and chop the tomatoes. Add them to the saucepan with the tomato paste, marjoram, and the seasoning. Then add the chick peas (garbanzo beans) and water, and stir well. Bring to the boil, then lower the heat and simmer, uncovered, for about 15 minutes.
4 Serve the stew over the rice.

* If making the whole week's menus then cook double this quantity of rice, cool and refrigerate half.

TUESDAY *Rich Nut Rissoles*

IMPERIAL/METRIC		AMERICAN
¾ oz (20g)	hard vegan margarine (e.g. Tomor)*	1½ tbs
1 oz (30g)	soya flour*	¼ cup
½–¾ tsp	yeast extract*	½–¾ tsp
2 oz (55g)	mixed nuts	½ cup
1 small	onion	1 small
1 tbs	vegetable oil (plus additional for frying rissoles)	1 tbs
1 tbs	wholemeal (whole wheat) flour	1 tbs
2 tbs	soya milk	2 tbs
1 oz (30g)	fresh wholemeal (wholewheat) breadcrumbs	½ cup
½ tsp	marjoram	½ tsp
	mixed salad ingredients	

1 Melt the margarine in a small saucepan over a low heat. Remove from the heat and stir in the soya flour and yeast extract. Pour the mixture onto an oiled flat tin or plate; cool, then chill until ready to use.
2 Grind the nuts.
3 Chop the onion finely. Sauté in the oil for 3–4 minutes. Stir in the flour and mix well, then add the milk and stir until thickened. Chop the soya flour mixture and stir it in as well.
4 Remove the pan from the heat and stir in the nuts, breadcrumbs and marjoram. Leave to cool while preparing the salad.
5 Form the mixture into three rissoles and shallow-fry in a little oil, turning once, so that both sides are browned. Serve with salad.

* If you made this on Sunday then simply use the refrigerated half of the mixture, skipping instruction 1 above.

WEDNESDAY *Mexican Chick Peas (Garbanzo Beans) and Bulgur Wheat*

IMPERIAL/METRIC		AMERICAN
1 small	onion	1 small
1 small clove	garlic	1 small clove
1 tbs	olive oil	1 tbs
½ tsp	ground cumin	½ tsp
½ tsp	oregano	½ tsp
½ tsp	paprika	½ tsp
⅛–¼ tsp	chilli powder	⅛–¼ tsp
2 small	tomatoes	2 small
1 tbs	tomato paste	1 tbs
½ x 15½ oz (440g) can	chick peas (garbanzo beans)	½ x 15½ oz can
3–5 tbs	water	3–5 tbs
2–2½ oz (55–70g)	bulgur wheat	⅓ cup

1 Chop the onion and crush the garlic. Sauté them in the oil for a few minutes. Add the cumin, oregano, paprika and chilli powder and stir over very low heat for a minute.
2 Skin and chop the tomatoes. Add them to the saucepan along with the tomato paste, the drained and rinsed chick peas (garbanzo beans), and the water. Bring to the boil, then lower the heat and simmer, uncovered, for 5–10 minutes, stirring occasionally.
3 Cover the bulgur wheat with about three times its quantity of water and a pinch of sea salt, bring to the boil, lower the heat, cover the pan and simmer until all the water is absorbed (only a few minutes).
4 Serve the chick peas (garbanzo beans) over the cooked bulgur wheat.

THURSDAY *Nasi Goreng*

IMPERIAL/METRIC		AMERICAN
2½–3 oz (70–85g)	brown rice	½ cup
3–4 oz (85–115g)	tofu	⅓–½ cup
1 tbs	vegan margarine	1 tbs
⅛	cucumber	⅛
1 small	onion	1 small
1 small clove	garlic	1 small clove
1 tbs	vegetable oil	1 tbs
1 tsp	ground coriander	1 tsp
1 tsp	ground cumin	1 tsp
1 tbs	mango chutney	1 tbs
2 tbs	Smokey Snaps (imitation bacon bits)	2 tbs

1 Cook the rice (or use rice which was cooked earlier in the week).
2 Slice the tofu into thin strips. Shallow-fry in the margarine in a frying pan (skillet) until lightly browned. Set aside (keep warm if convenient). Chop the cucumber finely. Set aside.
3 Chop the onion and garlic finely. Sauté them in the oil in a wok or frying pan (skillet) until beginning to turn brown. Lower the heat, add the spices and then the rice and stir well. Cook until the rice is heated through, then stir in the chutney and Smokey Snaps (imitation bacon bits).
4 Transfer to a plate and top with the tofu strips and cucumber.

Friday _Lentil and Vegetable Pottage_

IMPERIAL/METRIC		AMERICAN
1 small	onion	1 small
1 small clove	garlic	1 small clove
1 tbs	vegetable oil	1 tbs
3 oz (85g)	red lentils	½ cup
½ pint (285ml)	water	1⅓ cups
1	bay leaf	1
	sea salt and freshly ground black pepper to taste	
1 small	courgette (zucchini)	1 small
1 small	carrot	1 small
2 oz (55g)	mushrooms	1 cup
as required	wholemeal (whole wheat) bread	as required

1 Chop the onion. Crush the garlic. Sauté them in the oil in a saucepan for 2–3 minutes.
2 Add the lentils, water, bay leaf and seasoning. Bring to the boil, then lower the heat, cover the pan, and simmer for about 10 minutes.
3 Chop the courgette (zucchini), carrot and mushrooms quite finely. Add them to the saucepan, raise the heat until it is fully boiling again, then lower the heat, cover the pan, and simmer for a further 10 minutes.
4 Serve in a large bowl (a pottage is more substantial than a lunch-time soup but is eaten with a spoon) accompanied with the bread.

SATURDAY LUNCH *Chilled Cream of Tomato Soup*

IMPERIAL/METRIC		AMERICAN
1 small clove	garlic	1 small clove
1 tbs	vegan margarine	1 tbs
7 oz (200g) can	tomatoes	7 oz can
4 fl oz (115ml)	soya yogurt	½ cup
	freshly ground black pepper	

1 Chop the garlic finely. Sauté in the margarine until lightly browned.
2 Put all the ingredients in the liquidizer and blend thoroughly. Chill before serving.

Week 6

Shopping list

VEGETABLES AND FRUIT
Spring onions (scallions)
Parsley
Salad ingredients
Celery
Lemon
New potatoes
2 tomatoes
Fresh basil (sweet)
5 oz (140g) mushrooms
Seasonal green vegetable
2 small courgettes (zucchini)

MISCELLANEOUS
Ground almonds
Tofu
Tahini
Vegan chocolate
Vegan cream cheese
½ lb (225g) can butter (lima) beans
Cashews
Sun-dried tomatoes (in packet)
Sun-dried tomatoes (in oil)
Vegetarian Worcestershire sauce
Green lentils
Capers
Olives

Check that you have all the staples listed on pages xiii and xiv.

SUNDAY LUNCH *Nutty Salad**

IMPERIAL/METRIC		AMERICAN
1 small	spring onion (scallion)	1 small
1 oz (30g)	wholemeal (whole wheat) breadcrumbs	½ cup
1 oz (30g)	ground almonds	¼ cup
1–2 tsp	finely chopped parsley	1–2 tsp
2 tsp	tomato paste	2 tsp
1 tbs	water	1 tbs
	mixed salad ingredients	

1 Chop the spring onion (scallion) finely and put it in a bowl. Add the breadcrumbs, ground almonds, parsley, tomato paste and water. Mix well and press down in a small bowl. Put something on top of the mixture to weigh it down, and leave it in the fridge for a couple of hours.
2 Serve this on a bed of mixed salad ingredients. Wholemeal (whole wheat) toast is a nice accompaniment.

* A version of this recipe appeared in Leah Leneman's *Slim the Vegetarian Way*, now out of print.

SUNDAY DINNER *Tofu Celery Loaf**

IMPERIAL/METRIC		AMERICAN
1 oz (30g)	brown rice	⅙ cup
4–6 oz (115–170g)	tofu**	½–¾ cup
1 stick	celery	1 stick
1 oz (30g)	fresh wholemeal (whole wheat) breadcrumbs	½ cup
1 tbs	tahini	1 tbs
juice of ½ small	lemon	juice of ½ small
1 tbs	soya sauce	1 tbs
	seasonal vegetables e.g. spring cabbage (collards) or courgette (zucchini)	

1 Put the rice on to cook.
2 Drain and mash the tofu in a bowl.
3 Clean and chop the celery very finely. Add it to the bowl, as well as the breadcrumbs, tahini, lemon juice and soya sauce, and mix thoroughly. When the rice is cooked mix it in as well.
4 Transfer to a small loaf pan or baking dish, and bake at 375°F (190°C) Gas Mark 5 for 25–30 minutes. Alternatively, cover and microwave for 3 minutes.
5 Serve accompanied by a steamed seasonal vegetable.

* A version of this recipe appeared in Leah Leneman's *Slim the Vegetarian Way*, now out of print.
** If making the whole week's menus then slice and freeze 4–6 oz (115–170g) ½–¾ cup tofu.

SUNDAY DESSERT *Rich Chocolate Pudding*

IMPERIAL/METRIC		AMERICAN
1 oz (55g)	vegan chocolate	1 oz
2½ fl oz (100ml)	soya milk	⅓ cup
2 oz (55g)	vegan cream cheese	¼ cup
½ tsp	vanilla essence (extract)	½ tsp
1 oz (30g)	raw cane sugar	⅙ cup

1 Melt the chocolate in a small bowl over hot water.
2 Put all the ingredients into a liquidizer and blend thoroughly.
3 Pour into a serving bowl, refrigerate and leave for several hours.

MONDAY *Italian Rice with Butter (Lima) Beans and Potato*

IMPERIAL/METRIC		AMERICAN
2½ oz (70g)	brown rice	½ cup
1 clove	garlic	1 clove
1 small (2–3 oz/ 55–85g)	new potato	1 small (2–3 oz)
1 tbs	olive oil	1 tbs
1	tomato	1
2 tbs	tomato paste	2 tbs
2 tbs	water	2 tbs
1 tbs	fresh basil (sweet)	1 tbs
1 x 7½ oz (225g) can	butter (lima) beans	½ lb can
	sea salt and freshly ground black pepper to taste	
2 tsp	vegan Parmesan	2 tsp

1 Put the rice on to cook.
2 Skin and chop the garlic finely. Scrub and dice the potato into quite small pieces.
3 Heat the oil and sauté the garlic for a minute or two, until beginning to brown. Add the diced potato and cook for a couple of minutes longer.
4 Skin and chop the tomato and add it to the saucepan. Cook for a minute or two more, then add the tomato paste and water. Bring to the boil, then lower the heat, cover the pan, and leave to simmer, stirring occasionally.
5 Chop the basil finely. Drain and rinse the beans.
6 When the potato is tender stir in the basil and beans; heat thoroughly. Drain the cooked rice and stir it in.
7 Stir in one tsp of the vegan Parmesan, season to taste, and sprinkle the remaining vegan Parmesan on top.

TUESDAY *Mushroom and Cashew Savoury**

IMPERIAL/METRIC		AMERICAN
2 oz (55g)	whole cashews	½ cup
1 small	onion	1 small
1 small	tomato	1 small
3 oz (85g)	mushrooms	1½ cups
2 tsp	vegetable oil	2 tsp
1 tsp	wholemeal (whole wheat) flour	1 tsp
2½ fl oz (70ml)	water	⅓ cup
½ tsp	yeast extract	½ tsp
½ tsp	thyme	½ tsp
	freshly ground black pepper to taste	
	new potatoes as required	

1 Put the cashews under the grill (broiler); when lightly browned on one side flip them over and lightly brown them on the other side. Remove from the heat.
2 Skin and slice the onion thinly. Skin and slice the tomato. Clean and slice the mushrooms.
3 Heat the oil in a saucepan, and cook the vegetables for a few minutes, stirring frequently, until tender.
4 Stir in the flour, then slowly add the water, stirring constantly until thickened. Stir in the yeast extract, thyme and pepper, and then the cashews.
5 Serve accompanied with new potatoes.

* A version of this recipe appeared in Leah Leneman's *Slim the Vegetarian Way*, now out of print.

WEDNESDAY LUNCH *Spaghetti with Sun-Dried Tomatoes*

IMPERIAL/METRIC		AMERICAN
½ oz (15g)	sun-dried tomatoes*	½ oz
as required	boiling water	as required
3 oz (85g)	wholemeal (whole wheat) spaghetti	3 oz
1 clove	garlic	1 clove
3–4	black olives	3–4
1 tsp	red wine vinegar	1 tsp
1 tbs	olive oil	1 tbs
2 tsp	finely chopped fresh basil (sweet)	2 tsp
pinch	cayenne pepper	pinch
	sea salt and freshly ground black pepper to taste	

1 In the morning (or, at least, a good while earlier) put the sun-dried tomatoes into a bowl, pour boiling water over them, cover and leave to soak.
2 Drain the tomatoes and chop them coarsely. Put them in a microwave-proof container or a small saucepan.
3 Put the spaghetti on to cook.
4 Crush the garlic. Stone and chop the olives. Add these ingredients to the tomatoes, as well as the vinegar, oil, basil and cayenne. Mix well, and heat gently in a microwave or over a low heat.
5 Drain the spaghetti, return it to the pan, and stir in the tomato mixture. Season to taste and serve immediately.

* The kind in a packet, not the kind in oil in a jar.

THURSDAY *Tofu and Vegetables in Barbecue Sauce*

IMPERIAL/METRIC		AMERICAN
4–6 oz (115–170g)	sliced frozen tofu	½–¾ cup
2 tsp	vegan Worcestershire sauce	2 tsp
2 tsp	tomato paste	2 tsp
1 tsp	brown sugar	1 tsp
1 tsp	lemon juice	1 tsp
1 tsp	soya sauce	1 tsp
3 tbs	water	3 tbs
1 small	onion	1 small
1 clove	garlic	1 clove
2 tsp	vegetable oil	2 tsp
1 small	courgette (zucchini)	1 small
2 oz (55g)	mushrooms	1 cup
2–3 oz (55–85g)	bulgur wheat or couscous	½ cup

1 Thaw the frozen tofu slices and gently squeeze out any liquid.
2 Combine in a bowl the Worcestershire sauce, tomato paste, sugar, lemon juice, soya sauce and water. Put the tofu slices into the bowl and leave to marinate.
3 Chop the onion and garlic. Heat the oil in a saucepan and sauté, for about 3 minutes, until tenderized.
4 Dice the courgette (zucchini). Slice the mushrooms. Add them to the pan, and cook until just tender.
5 Meanwhile, prepare the bulgur wheat or couscous.
6 Add the tofu slices and barbecue sauce to the vegetables, and stir until thoroughly heated. Serve over the bulgur wheat or couscous.

FRIDAY *Frying Pan Pizza*

IMPERIAL/METRIC		AMERICAN
1 small	onion	1 small
1 clove	garlic	1 clove
3 tsp	olive oil	3 tsp
1 small	courgette (zucchini)	1 small
1	sun-dried tomato in oil	1
2–3	black olives	2–3
1 tsp	oregano	1 tsp
2–3 oz (55–85g)	wholemeal (whole wheat) flour	½–⅔ cup
¼ tsp	baking powder	¼ tsp
pinch	sea salt	pinch
water as required
2–3 tsp	tomato paste	2–3 tsp
1 tbs	vegan Parmesan	1 tbs
freshly ground black pepper to taste

1 Chop the onion and garlic finely. Heat 2 tsp of the oil in a frying pan (skillet), and sauté, for 2–3 minutes. Dice the courgette (zucchini), add it to the pan, and fry for a further 3–4 minutes.

2 Remove the vegetables from the frying pan (skillet), and wipe the pan dry. Chop the sun-dried tomato and olives finely, and mix them in, along with the oregano.

3 Mix the flour (the larger amount for a thick crust; the smaller amount for a thin one), baking powder and salt in a bowl. Add water a tbs at a time until a dough can be formed. Place this on a floured board and roll out to make a base.

4 Heat the remaining 1 tsp oil in a frying pan (skillet), and fry the base over a low to medium heat for 3–5 minutes, then turn it over and fry for a couple of minutes longer.

5 Spread the tomato paste over the base, then top with the vegetables. Sprinkle with vegan Parmesan and pepper, and place under a hot grill (broiler) for 3–5 minutes. Serve immediately.

SATURDAY LUNCH *Green Lentil Salad*

IMPERIAL/METRIC		AMERICAN
2 oz (55g)	green lentils	½ cup
1 small	onion	1 small
1	bay leaf	1
1–2 tsp	capers	1–2 tsp
2 tsp	olive oil	2 tsp
1 tsp	wine vinegar	1 tsp
	sea salt and freshly ground black pepper to taste	
	fresh lettuce leaves	

1 Chop the onion finely. Wash the lentils and put them in a small saucepan; cover with cold water, the chopped onion, bay leaf, and a little salt. Cover, bring to the boil, then lower the heat and simmer until tender.
2 Chop the capers finely. When the lentils are tender and the water is absorbed, remove the pan from the heat, and stir in the chopped capers, oil and vinegar, and season to taste. Leave to cool, then refrigerate.
3 Taste for seasoning, and add more salt or pepper if necessary. Serve on a bed of fresh lettuce leaves with wholemeal (whole wheat) bread.

Week 7

Shopping list

VEGETABLES AND FRUIT
6–7 oz (170–200g) young
  spinach
3–4 oz (85–115g) button
  mushrooms
Spring onions (scallions)
5 small onions
Garlic
Small tomato
New potatoes
Small leek
Small carrot
Lemon
Beansprouts
Spring cabbage (collards)
Cucumber
¼-inch fresh ginger
Small courgette (zucchini)
1 small red and 1 red or
  1 green pepper
Salad ingredients

MISCELLANEOUS
Walnuts
Olives
Sun-dried tomatoes in oil
Green lentils
Couscous
Ground almonds
Split red lentils
Rose and/or orange
  blossom water
Rolled oats
Tofu
Creamed coconut
Tabasco sauce
Eggless Chinese noodles
Yellow bean sauce
Flaked (slivered) almonds

Check that you have all the staples listed on pages xiii and xiv.

Spinach, Walnut and Mushroom Salad

IMPERIAL/METRIC		AMERICAN
2–3 oz (55–85g)	young spinach leaves	2–3 oz
2 oz (55g)	walnut halves or pieces	½ cup
2 oz (55g)	button mushrooms	1 cup
3–4	olives	3–4
1 tbs	olive oil	1 tbs
1½ tsp	wine vinegar	1½ tsp
1 tsp	vegan Parmesan	1 tsp
	sea salt and freshly ground black pepper to taste	

1 Wash the spinach (if not already washed), and drain well.
2 Clean and slice the mushrooms. Chop the olives finely.
3 Put all of the ingredients in a bowl – because of the nature of spinach leaves it will have to be a ridiculously large bowl – and mix thoroughly.
4 Taste for seasoning and serve, if desired, with a crusty wholemeal (whole wheat) roll.

Stuffed Pepper

IMPERIAL/METRIC		AMERICAN
1 oz (30g)	green lentils	1 oz
1	red or green pepper	1
1 small	onion	1 small
1 clove	garlic	1 clove
2 tsp	vegetable oil	2 tsp
1 small	tomato	1 small
1–2 oz (30–55g)	mushrooms	½–1 cup
1 tbs fresh	marjoram	1 tbs fresh
or 1 tsp dried		or 1 tsp dried
2 tsp	soya sauce	2 tsp
2 tsp	tomato paste	2 tsp
1 oz (30g)	couscous	¼ cup
	sea salt and freshly ground	
	black pepper to taste	
	boiled or roasted new potatoes	

1 Cover the lentils with lots of cold water in a saucepan, add a little sea salt, cover the pan, bring to the boil, then lower the heat and leave to simmer until tender (20–30 minutes).
2 Halve and de-seed the pepper. Put the halves into a bowl or saucepan of boiling water, remove from the heat, cover and leave for about 5 minutes. Drain.

3   Chop the onion and garlic finely. Heat the oil in a frying pan (skillet), and sauté, for about 3 minutes.
4   Skin and chop the tomato. Clean and chop the mushrooms. Add them to the frying pan (skillet), and cook for a few minutes longer.
5   Remove the frying pan (skillet) from the heat, and add the marjoram, soya sauce and tomato paste.
6   When the lentils are soft, make sure there is at least ¼-inch (6mm) water left in the pan (add more if necessary). Put the couscous in, cover the pan and leave for about 3 minutes. If the water has not all been absorbed then bring to the boil and simmer, uncovered, until it has. Mix the lentils and couscous with the contents of the frying pan (skillet). Add seasoning to taste.
7   Put the pepper halves into a casserole and pile the stuffing into them. Cover with foil or a lid and bake at 375°F (190°C) Gas Mark 5 for about half an hour. Alternatively, cover with greaseproof paper and microwave for 3 minutes.
8   Serve accompanied by boiled or roasted new potatoes.

SUNDAY DESSERT *Middle-Eastern Pudding*

IMPERIAL/METRIC		AMERICAN
8 fl oz (¼ litre)	soya milk	1 cup
1 tbs	cornflour (cornstarch)	1 tbs
1–2 tbs	raw cane sugar	1–2 tbs
1 oz (30g)	ground almonds	¼ cup
1 tsp	orange blossom water and	1 tsp
1 tsp	rose water	1 tsp
	or	
2 tsp	of either	2 tsp
1 tbs	flaked (slivered) almonds	1 tbs

1 Mix a little of the milk with the cornflour (cornstarch) while bringing the rest to the boil in a saucepan. Pour the boiling milk into the cornflour (cornstarch) mixture, stir well, then return it to the pan and stir until thickened. Add sugar, taste for sweetness, and cook for a minute or so longer.
2 Remove from the heat and stir in the ground almonds and orange blossom water and/or rose water. Leave to cool, then chill in the fridge. Sprinkle with chopped almonds before serving.

MONDAY *Summer Stew**

IMPERIAL/METRIC		AMERICAN
1 small	onion	1 small
1 small	leek	1 small
2 tsp	vegetable oil	2 tsp
1 small	carrot	1 small
2 oz (55g)	split red lentils	½ cup
4 oz (115g)	fresh spinach	4 oz
2–3 tbs	rolled oats	2–3 tbs
	sea salt and freshly ground black pepper to taste	
	new potatoes	

1 Peel and chop the onion. Clean and chop the leek. Heat the oil in a saucepan, and sauté the onion and leek for 2–3 minutes. Slice the carrot, add it to the pan, and cook for a further 2–3 minutes.
2 Wash the lentils and add them to the pan, along with enough water to cover them well. Sprinkle in a little sea salt. Wash the spinach (if not already washed), chop it coarsely, and add it to the pan. When everything is boiling, lower the heat, cover the pan, and leave to simmer for about 10–15 minutes, until everything is tender.
3 Stir in the oats and cook, uncovered, for a few minutes longer, until thick and creamy. Taste for seasoning and add more if required.
4 Serve with boiled new potatoes.

* A version of this recipe appeared in Leah Leneman's *Slim the Vegetarian Way*, now out of print.

TUESDAY *Gado-Gado*

IMPERIAL/METRIC		AMERICAN
4–5 oz (115–140g)	tofu	½–⅔ cup
3 tsp	vegetable oil	3 tsp
1 small	onion	1 small
2 cloves	garlic	2 cloves
½ oz (15g)	creamed coconut	½ oz
2–3 tsp	peanut butter	2–3 tsp
1–2 tsp	grated lemon rind	1–2 tsp
2 tsp	lemon juice	2 tsp
½ tsp	Tabasco sauce	½ tsp
(or to taste)		(or to taste)
½ tsp	raw cane sugar	½ tsp
1 tsp	soya sauce	1 tsp
3–4 tbs	hot water	3–4 tbs
3 oz (85g)	beansprouts	3 oz
2–3 oz (55–85g)	spring cabbage (collards)	2–3 oz
few slices	cucumber	few slices
as required	wholemeal (whole wheat) bread or brown rice	as required

1 Dice the tofu. Heat half the oil in a frying pan (skillet), and sauté the pieces until turning golden. Remove from the heat and keep warm (or re-heat at the end).
2 Chop the onion and garlic finely. Heat the remaining oil in a small saucepan, and sauté them for about 3 minutes.
3 Grate the creamed coconut.
4 Remove the saucepan from the heat, and add the creamed coconut, peanut butter, lemon rind and juice, Tabasco sauce, sugar, soya sauce, and water. Return the pan to a gentle heat, and stir constantly until it is a nice thick sauce.
5 Shred the cabbage and blanch it and the beansprouts in boiling water for a minute or two; drain well.
6 Arrange the greens, beansprouts, and cucumber slices on a plate, top with the tofu cubes, and pour the sauce over the whole. Either serve it accompanied with bread or on top of steamed rice.

WEDNESDAY *Dhal with Courgettes (Zucchini)*

IMPERIAL/METRIC		AMERICAN
2 oz (55g)	split red lentils	½ cup
	sea salt to taste	
¼ tsp	turmeric	¼ tsp
1 small	onion	1 small
1 clove	garlic	1 clove
3 tsp	vegetable oil	3 tsp
¼-inch piece	fresh ginger	¼-inch piece
1 small	courgette (zucchini)	1 small
½ tsp	garam masala	½ tsp
¼ tsp	chilli powder	¼ tsp
1 tsp	cumin seeds	1 tsp
1 tsp	grated creamed coconut	1 tsp
	cooked brown rice plus (if desired)	
	poppadum or chapati	

1 Wash the lentils and cover with cold water in a small saucepan. Add a little salt and the turmeric. Cover the pan, bring to the boil, then lower the heat and simmer, adding more water if necessary so that the lentils do not dry out.
2 Chop the onion and garlic. Heat 2 tsp of the oil in a larger saucepan, and sauté them for 2–3 minutes.
3 Peel and chop the ginger finely. Clean and slice the courgette (zucchini). Add these to the onion and garlic, and stir-fry for a couple of minutes longer.
4 Transfer the lentils (which should, by now, be nearly cooked but still retain some water) to the pan, and add the garam masala and chilli powder. Cover and cook over a very low heat for a few minutes longer.
5 Meanwhile heat the remaining oil in a small frying pan (skillet), and add the cumin seeds. When they start to sizzle and change colour remove from the heat.
6 Stir the creamed coconut into the lentil mixture and top with the cumin seeds. Serve over rice, accompanied, if desired, with a poppadum or chapati.

THURSDAY *Noodles with Tofu and Yellow Bean Sauce*

IMPERIAL/METRIC		AMERICAN
2 oz (55g)	eggless noodles	2 oz
1 small	onion	1 small
½ small	red pepper	½ small
1 clove	garlic	1 clove
2 tsp	vegetable oil	2 tsp
2–3 oz (55–85g)	beansprouts	2–3 oz
4–5 oz (115–140g)	tofu	½–⅔ cup
2–3 tsp	yellow bean sauce*	2–3 tsp
few drops	Tabasco sauce	few drops

1 Cook the noodles according to the packet instructions and drain thoroughly.
2 Peel and slice the onion thinly. De-seed and slice the red pepper thinly. Chop the garlic finely.
3 Heat the oil in a wok and add the onion, red pepper, garlic and beansprouts. Stir-fry for about 2 minutes.
4 Put the tofu into a tea towel (dish towel) and squeeze out as much liquid as possible. Put the dry tofu into the wok and stir-fry for a minute or two longer.
5 Add the noodles, yellow bean sauce and Tabasco sauce, and stir-fry until well mixed and thoroughly heated. Serve immediately.

* Available in most supermarkets.

FRIDAY *Spaghetti with Red Pesto Sauce*

IMPERIAL/METRIC		AMERICAN
½ small	red pepper	½ small
3 oz (85g)	wholemeal (whole wheat) spaghetti	3 oz
1	spring onion (scallion)	1
1 clove	garlic	1 clove
2	sun-dried tomatoes in oil	2
½ oz (15g)	toasted flaked (slivered) almonds	½ oz
1 tsp	olive oil	1 tsp
2 tsp	vegan Parmesan	2 tsp
2 tsp	water	2 tsp
	salad ingredients	

1   De-seed and halve the red pepper. Place under a hot grill (broiler), outside uppermost, and cook until well charred. Remove from the heat and leave to cool.
2   Put the spaghetti on to cook.
3   Chop the spring onion (scallion) and garlic finely. Drain the tomatoes and chop them. Put these ingredients into a small food processor or blender, and add the almonds, oil, vegan Parmesan and water. Blend thoroughly.
4   When the spaghetti is cooked, drain it and pour the pesto into the saucepan. Return the spaghetti to the pan over a very low heat and mix well. Serve immediately, accompanied with a green salad.

SATURDAY LUNCH *Chilled Cucumber Soup*

IMPERIAL/METRIC		AMERICAN
4–6 oz (115–170g)	cucumber	4–6 oz
2–3	spring onions (scallions)	2–3
8 fl oz (¼ litre) plus 2 tsp	water	1 cup + 2 tsp
1 tsp	cornflour (cornstarch)	1 tsp
1 tbs	soya cream	1 tbs
	sea salt and freshly ground black pepper to taste	
	freshly ground nutmeg	

1 Peel and dice the cucumber. Chop the spring onions (scallions) finely. Put them in a saucepan with the 8 fl oz (¼ litre/1 cup) water, cover, bring to the boil, then lower the heat and simmer for 10–15 minutes.
2 Remove from the heat, cool briefly, then put in a liquidizer and blend (the texture is more appealing if not completely smooth). Return to the saucepan and a low heat.
3 Mix the cornflour (cornstarch) with 2 tsp of water in a cup. Pour in a little of the hot soup, mix well, then return to the saucepan and bring to the boil, stirring constantly. Simmer for a minute or two, then remove from the heat.
4 Stir in the soya cream, salt, pepper and nutmeg. Cool, then chill. Taste for seasoning before serving. Wholemeal (whole wheat) toast as an accompaniment provides a nice contrast of textures.

Week 8

Shopping list

VEGETABLES AND FRUIT

Peas (1oz/30g)
Celery
Lettuce
4 small onions
Garlic
4–6 oz (115–170g) tomatoes
2 small courgettes (zucchini)
Fresh basil (sweet)
Strawberries
6 oz (170g) button mushrooms
Small red pepper
6–8 oz (170–225g) potatoes
Aubergine (eggplant)
Seasonal vegetables
Lemon

MISCELLANEOUS

Vegan 'chicken' slices
Vegan sour cream
Vegan chocolate
Flaked (slivered) almonds
Walnuts
Cashews
Small [about 7 oz (230g)]
can tomatoes

Check that you have all the staples listed on pages xiii and xiv.

SUNDAY LUNCH 'Chicken' Salad

IMPERIAL/METRIC		AMERICAN
1 oz (30g)	shelled peas	1 oz
about 2 oz (50g)	vegan 'chicken' slices	about 2 oz
1 stick	celery	1 stick
2 tsp	vegan mayonnaise	2 tsp
2 tsp	vegan sour cream	2 tsp
	lettuce leaves	

1 Cook the peas until just tender. Drain and cool.
2 Coarsely chop the 'chicken' slices. Clean and chop the celery. Combine these ingredients in a bowl with the peas, mayonnaise and sour cream.
3 Serve on a bed of shredded lettuce, accompanied with wholemeal (whole wheat) bread.

*Pasta al Forno**

IMPERIAL/METRIC		AMERICAN
2½–3 oz (70–85g)	pasta shapes (e.g. penne or shells)	2½–3 oz
1 small	onion	1 small
1 clove	garlic	1 clove
2 tsp	olive oil	2 tsp
4–6 oz (115–170g)	tomatoes	4–6 oz
1 small	courgette (zucchini)	1 small
1 tbs	chopped fresh basil (sweet)	1 tbs
	sea salt and freshly ground black pepper to taste	
1–2 tsp	vegan margarine	1–2 tsp
1–2 tbs	vegan Parmesan	1–2 tbs

1 Cook the pasta until just tender, and drain.
2 Meanwhile, chop the onion and crush the garlic. Heat the oil in a saucepan, and sauté until just beginning to brown.
3 Skin and chop the tomatoes. Dice the courgette (zucchini). Add these to the saucepan, cover the pan, lower the heat, and leave to simmer for about 5 minutes.
4 Remove from the heat, add the basil and seasoning, and mix with the cooked, drained pasta.
5 Transfer to an oiled baking dish, top with the margarine and vegan Parmesan, and bake at 375°F (190°C) Gas Mark 5 for about 20 minutes.

* A version of this recipe appeared in Leah Leneman's *Slim the Vegetarian Way*, now out of print.

SUNDAY DESSERT *Strawberries with Chocolate Topping*

IMPERIAL/METRIC		AMERICAN
4–5 oz (115–140g)	fresh strawberries	4–5 oz
¾ oz (20g)	vegan chocolate	¾ oz
2 tsp	icing (confectioner's) sugar	2 tsp
1 tbs	soya cream	1 tbs

1   Wash, hull and dry the strawberries and put them in a serving bowl.
2   Break up the chocolate and put it into a small bowl. Boil some water in a saucepan; remove from the heat and place the bowl with the chocolate pieces into the hot water. Leave for a few minutes (or while eating the main course) until the chocolate has melted.
3   Stir the sugar and cream into the melted chocolate, and spoon on top of the strawberries. Serve immediately.

MONDAY 'Chicken' Spaghetti Casserole

IMPERIAL/METRIC		AMERICAN
2½ oz (70g)	wholemeal (whole wheat) spaghetti	2½ oz
½ oz (15g)	flaked (slivered) almonds	½ oz
3 oz (85g)	button mushrooms	1½ cups
½ small	red pepper	½ small
1 tbs	vegan margarine	1 tbs
1 tbs	wholemeal (whole wheat) flour	1 tbs
4 fl oz (115ml)	soya milk	½ cup
about 2 oz (50g)	vegan 'chicken' slices	about 2 oz
	sea salt and freshly ground	
	black pepper to taste	
1 oz (30g)	wholemeal (whole wheat) breadcrumbs	½ cup
2 tsp	vegan Parmesan	2 tsp

1 Break the spaghetti into three. Cook until just tender.
2 Put the almonds under the grill (broiler) until lightly browned.
3 Wipe and slice the mushrooms. De-seed and chop the red pepper.
4 Heat the margarine in a saucepan, and sauté the mushrooms and red pepper for about 3 minutes. Stir in the flour, then slowly add the soya milk, stirring constantly until thickened.
5 Dice the 'chicken' slices and add them to the pan, stirring until warmed.
6 Mix together the drained spaghetti, toasted flaked (slivered) almonds, and the sauce, and transfer the mixture to a casserole dish. Season and top with the breadcrumbs and vegan Parmesan. Place under a grill (broiler) or in a hot oven until lightly browned. (If the ingredients have not been kept piping hot, then after the top is browned the casserole can be briefly heated in a microwave.) Serve immediately.

TUESDAY *Indian-Style Courgettes (Zucchini) and Peppers*

IMPERIAL/METRIC		AMERICAN
2½–3 oz (70–85g)	brown rice*	⅓–½ cup
1 small	onion	1 small
1 clove	garlic	1 clove
1 tbs	vegan margarine	1 tbs
¼ tsp	turmeric	¼ tsp
¼ tsp	chilli powder (cayenne pepper)	¼ tsp
1 tsp	garam masala	1 tsp
1 small	courgette (zucchini)	1 small
½ small	red pepper	½ small
3 oz (85ml)	soya yogurt	⅓ cup
1 tbs	water	1 tbs
	sea salt to taste	

1 Put the rice on to cook.
2 Slice the onion thinly. Chop the garlic finely. Heat the margarine in a large saucepan, and sauté for about 5 minutes. Stir in the turmeric, chilli powder (cayenne pepper) and garam masala, and cook for a minute or so longer, over a low heat.
3 Slice the courgette (zucchini). De-seed and thinly slice the red pepper. Add them to the pan, and stir-fry for a couple of minutes more. Add the yogurt, water and salt. Bring to the boil, then lower the heat, cover the pan, and leave to simmer for about 10 minutes.
4 Serve over the rice, accompanied by a chapati or poppadum if desired.

---

* If preparing the whole week's menus, then cook an extra 1 oz (30g) brown rice, separate it out, leave to cool, and then refrigerate it.

WEDNESDAY *Aubergine (Eggplant) with Potato Sauce*

IMPERIAL/METRIC		AMERICAN
6–8 oz (170–225g)	potatoes	6–8 oz
1 tbs	olive oil	1 tbs
1 tbs	wine vinegar	1 tbs
1 clove	garlic	1 clove
	sea salt and freshly ground black pepper to taste	
1 [about 8 oz (225g)]	aubergine (eggplant)	1 (about ½ lb)
as required	wholemeal (whole wheat) flour	as required
as required	vegan margarine	as required

1 Boil the potatoes until tender. Drain and mash (peeled first if preferred). Stir in the oil and vinegar. Crush the garlic and add it to the mixture. Season to taste. Keep this warm.
2 In the meantime slice the aubergine (eggplant) thinly. Season some flour on a plate and dip the slices into the flour.
3 Heat some margarine in a frying pan (skillet), and fry the aubergine (eggplant) slices until lightly browned on both sides. (This will probably have to be done in two instalments, keeping the first lot warm while frying the second.)
4 Serve the slices topped with the potato sauce.

THURSDAY *Creamy Pasta with Mushrooms and Walnuts*

IMPERIAL/METRIC		AMERICAN
1 small	onion	1 small
2 tsp	olive oil	2 tsp
1 clove	garlic	1 clove
3 oz (85g)	button mushrooms	1½ cups
2½–3 oz (70–85g)	pasta shapes (e.g. penne or shells)	2½–3 oz
½–1 oz (15–30g)	walnuts	⅛–¼ cup
1 tsp	cornflour (cornstarch)	1 tsp
3 fl oz (85ml)	soya cream	⅓ cup
	sea salt and freshly ground	
	black pepper to taste	
	salad ingredients	

1 Chop the onion finely. Heat the oil in a saucepan, and sauté for about 3 minutes.
2 Crush the garlic and clean and slice the mushrooms. Add them to the pan, lower the heat, cover the pan, and leave to simmer for about 10 minutes.
3 Cook the pasta. Chop the walnuts.
4 Sprinkle the cornflour (cornstarch) on the mushroom mixture, then stir in the soya cream until thickened and heated. Season well and stir in the walnuts.
5 Drain the pasta and stir it into the creamy sauce. Serve accompanied with a salad.

FRIDAY Cashew-Rice Patties

IMPERIAL/METRIC   AMERICAN

IMPERIAL/METRIC		AMERICAN
1 small	onion	1 small
2 tsp	olive oil	2 tsp
1 stick	celery	1 stick
1 oz (30g)	wholemeal (whole wheat) breadcrumbs	½ cup
1 oz (30g)	brown rice, cooked	⅙ cup
1 oz (30g)	cashew nuts	¼ cup
2 fl oz (55ml)	water	¼ cup
½ tsp	oregano	½ tsp
1 tsp	soya sauce	1 tsp
	sea salt and freshly ground black pepper to taste	
	seasonal vegetables	

1 Chop the onion finely. Heat the oil in a saucepan and sauté for about 3–4 minutes, until beginning to brown. Remove from the heat.
2 Chop the celery very finely and add it to the saucepan, along with the breadcrumbs and cooked rice.
3 Grind the cashews, then add the water and liquidize thoroughly. Add this to the rest of the ingredients, along with the oregano, soya sauce, and seasoning.
4 Oil a baking (cookie) sheet. Spoon 3 patties onto the sheet and flatten slightly (don't worry about the fact that they are runny; they won't stay like that).
5 Bake at 425°F (210°C) Gas Mark 7 for 20 minutes, by which time they should be lightly browned. Serve accompanied with steamed seasonal vegetables.

SATURDAY LUNCH *Chilled Summer Soup**

IMPERIAL/METRIC		AMERICAN
1 small (230g) can	tomatoes	7 oz can
2 oz (55g)	soya yogurt	¼ cup
2 tsp	olive oil	2 tsp
1 tsp	lemon juice	1 tsp
1 tbs	chopped fresh basil (sweet)	1 tbs
	freshly ground black pepper to taste	

1 Put all the ingredients into a liquidizer and blend thoroughly.
2 Chill before serving. (Alternatively, if all the ingredients have been well chilled beforehand, serve immediately.) Nice with crusty wholemeal (whole wheat) or Italian-style bread.

* A version of this recipe appeared in Leah Leneman's, *Slim the Vegetarian Way*, now out of print.

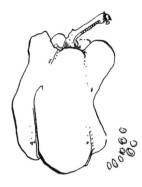

Week 9

Shopping list

VEGETABLES AND FRUIT
1 small green pepper
1 large + 4 oz (115g) tomatoes
2 courgettes (zucchini)
Spring onions (scallions)
6 oz (115g) mushrooms
3 oz (85g) sweetcorn –
   fresh, frozen or canned
1 lemon
1 large ripe peach
Lettuce
1 small carrot
2–3 oz (55–85g) fresh green
   beans
Fresh ginger root
3 small onions
2 oz (55g) shelled peas
Good handful of at least 4
   different fresh summer herbs
   (e.g. mint, marjoram, parsley,
   chives)

MISCELLANEOUS
Millet
Hard vegan cheese
Eggless Chinese noodles
Desiccated (shredded)
   coconut
Tofu
Roasted cashews
1 14 oz (420g) can haricot
   (navy)/cannellini (great
   northern) beans
Sesame oil

Check that you have all the staples listed on pages xiii and xiv.

SUNDAY LUNCH Creamy Vegetables on Toast

IMPERIAL/METRIC		AMERICAN
1 small	onion	1 small
½ small	green pepper	½ small
4 oz (115g)	ripe tomatoes	¼ lb
2 tsp	vegan margarine	2 tsp
1 tsp	finely chopped fresh basil (sweet)	1 tsp
	sea salt and freshly ground black pepper to taste	
2 fl oz (55g)	soya cream	¼ cup
1 tsp	wholemeal (whole wheat) flour	1 tsp
as required	wholemeal (whole wheat) toast	as required

1 Chop the onion, de-seeded green pepper, and tomatoes finely.
2 Heat the margarine in a saucepan, and stir in the vegetables. Cover the pan, reduce the heat to very low, and leave to cook for 15–20 minutes, stirring occasionally. Remove from the heat and add the basil and seasoning.
3 In a separate small saucepan combine the cream and flour and heat gently until beginning to thicken.
4 Stir the vegetables into the cream, re-heat gently, taste for seasoning, and serve over hot toast.

SUNDAY DINNER

Millet and Vegetable Gratin

IMPERIAL/METRIC		AMERICAN
2 oz (55g)	millet	½ cup
6 fl oz (170ml)	water	¾ cup
	sea salt and freshly ground black pepper to taste	
2	spring onions (scallions)	2
1 small	courgette (zucchini)	1 small
1 stick	celery (optional)	1 stick
2 tsp	vegetable oil	2 tsp
2 oz (55g)	mushrooms	1 cup
3 oz (85g)	cooked sweetcorn fresh, frozen or canned	½ cup
grated rind of ½ small	lemon	grated rind of ½ small
2 tsp	vegan margarine	2 tsp
2 tsp	wholemeal (whole wheat) flour	2 tsp
3 fl oz (85ml)	soya milk	⅓ cup
2 oz (55g)	hard vegan cheese	2 oz

1 Dry-roast the millet briefly in a heavy-bottomed pan until there is a slightly toasted smell to it, then add the water and a pinch of sea salt. Cover the pan and bring to the boil. Lower the heat, and leave to simmer for 15–20 minutes, until tender and the water is absorbed.

2 Meanwhile chop the spring onions (scallions), courgette (zucchini), and celery (if using) finely. Heat the oil in a saucepan, and sauté the vegetables. Clean and chop the mushrooms finely, add to the pan, and sauté for a few minutes longer, until the vegetables are crisp-tender. Stir in the sweetcorn.

3 Remove the vegetables from the heat; add the grated lemon rind and seasoning to taste.

4 Heat the margarine in a small pan, and stir in the flour, and then the soya milk, until smooth; simmer for a minute or so, then remove from the heat.

5 Mix together the millet, vegetables and sauce. Grate the vegan cheese, and mix in half. Transfer the mixture to a baking dish, and top with the remainder of the cheese.

6 Bake at 350°F (180°C) Gas Mark 4 for about 20 minutes, or alternatively microwave for 2 minutes.

SUNDAY DESSERT Grilled (Broiled) Spiced Peach

IMPERIAL/METRIC		AMERICAN
1 large	ripe peach	1 large
1 tbs	raw cane sugar	1 tbs
pinch	cinnamon	pinch
grating of	nutmeg	grating of
1 tsp	vegan margarine	1 tsp
	vegan sour cream, soya cream or soya yogurt	

1 Cover the peach with boiling water, leave for a minute, then drain, cool and skin.
2 Slice the peach thickly and place it in a flameproof dish. Sprinkle with sugar, cinnamon and nutmeg, and dot with margarine.
3 Place under a hot grill (broiler) for about 5 minutes until sizzling hot. Serve immediately, with vegan sour cream or soya cream or yogurt.

MONDAY *Indonesian Noodles*

IMPERIAL/METRIC		AMERICAN
1 tbs	desiccated (shredded) coconut	1 tbs
3 oz (85g)	outer lettuce leaves*	3 oz (85g)
½-inch piece	fresh ginger root	½-inch piece
½ small	green pepper	½ small
1 tbs	peanut butter	1 tbs
2 tbs	soya milk	2 tbs
2 tsp	soya sauce	2 tsp
2½–3 oz (70–85g)	eggless noodles	2½–3 oz
2 tsp	vegetable oil	2 tsp
	sea salt and freshly ground black pepper to taste	

1 Put the coconut under the grill (broiler) and toast until just beginning to brown. Set aside.
2 Wash the lettuce leaves, pat them dry with kitchen (paper) towels, and chop coarsely. Set aside.
3 Peel and chop the ginger finely. De-seed and slice the green pepper very thinly. Set aside.
4 Blend the peanut butter, soya milk and soya sauce in a liquidizer. Set aside.
5 Cook the noodles according to the packet directions, and drain them.
6 Heat the oil in a wok and stir-fry the ginger and green pepper for a minute or two. Add the chopped lettuce and stir-fry for a further minute or two. Then add the noodles and toss well together. Stir in the peanut butter sauce, and heat thoroughly. Season to taste and serve immediately, topped with the toasted coconut.

* The heart of the lettuce can be saved for a salad. If it is a large lettuce with lots of coarse outer leaves, then it can also be used for Thursday dinner.

TUESDAY *Tofu with Cashews and Vegetables*

IMPERIAL/METRIC		AMERICAN
1 small	carrot	1 small
2–3 oz (55–85g)	fresh green beans	2–3 oz
2	spring onions (scallions)	2
4–5 oz (115–170g)	tofu	½–⅔ cup
1 tbs	vegetable oil	1 tbs
1 tsp	finely grated fresh ginger root	1 tsp
1 tbs	soya sauce	1 tbs
2 tbs	water	2 tbs
½ tsp	raw cane sugar	½ tsp
½ tsp	cornflour (cornstarch)	½ tsp
1 oz (30g)	roasted cashews	¼ cup
2½–3 oz (70–85g)	brown rice*	½ cup

1 Cut the carrot into thin sticks. Top, tail and coarsely chop the beans. Set aside.
2 Chop the spring onions (scallions) finely. Set aside.
3 Dice the tofu. Heat half the oil in a wok, and stir-fry the tofu for a couple of minutes, until beginning to turn golden. Remove from the wok.
4 Heat the remaining oil and add the chopped spring onions (scallions) and grated ginger. Stir-fry for a minute or two, then add the beans and carrot. Continue stir-frying for 2–3 minutes longer.
5 Combine the soya sauce, water and sugar in a cup, and whisk in the cornflour (cornstarch). Add this to the wok, and simmer until the beans are crisp-tender.
6 Add the tofu and cashews to the wok, and serve over brown rice when everything is piping hot.

* If making the whole week's menus, then cook double this quantity of rice, cool and refrigerate half of it.

WEDNESDAY *Macaroni with Courgette (Zucchini) and Beans*

IMPERIAL/METRIC		AMERICAN
2–3 oz (55–85g)	macaroni	⅓–½ cup
1 small	onion	1 small
1 clove	garlic	1 clove
1 tbs	olive oil	1 tbs
1 small	courgette (zucchini)	1 small
2 tbs	tomato paste	2 tbs
3 fl oz (85ml)	water	⅓ cup
½ 14 oz (420g) can	haricot (navy)/cannellini (great northern) beans	½ 14 oz can
3 or 4 leaves	fresh basil (sweet)	3 or 4 leaves
1 tbs	chopped fresh parsley	1 tbs
2 tsp	vegan Parmesan	2 tsp

1 Cook the macaroni according to the packet instructions.
2 Chop the onion. Crush the garlic. Heat the oil in a large saucepan, and sauté them for about 3 minutes.
3 Slice the courgette (zucchini) and add it to the pan. Sauté for about 2 minutes.
4 Add the tomato paste and water, and bring to the boil. Lower the heat, and simmer for 2–3 minutes.
5 Drain and rinse the beans. Chop the basil finely. Add the beans, basil, and parsley to the saucepan, and simmer for 3–4 minutes longer.
6 Mix the drained, cooked macaroni into the sauce. Stir in 1 tsp of the vegan Parmesan. Serve immediately, sprinkled with the remaining tsp of vegan Parmesan.

THURSDAY 'Cheesy' Rice Savoury

IMPERIAL/METRIC		AMERICAN
1 small	onion	1 small
1 tbs	vegetable oil	1 tbs
2 oz (55g)	mushrooms	1 cup
1 large	ripe tomato	1 large
2 oz (55g)	shelled peas	2 oz
2½–3 oz (70–85g)	brown rice, cooked	½ cup
2 oz (55g)	hard vegan cheese	2 oz
	sea salt and freshly ground black pepper to taste	

1   Chop the onion. Heat the oil in a large frying pan (skillet) and sauté the onion for about 2 minutes.
2   Clean and chop the mushrooms. Add them to the frying pan (skillet) and cook for another minute or two.
3   Skin and slice the tomato and add it to the frying pan (skillet). Cook for a couple of minutes longer. Add the peas and cook until they are just tender.
4   Stir in the cooked rice. Grate the cheese and stir it in as well. Continue cooking until the mixture is piping hot. Season to taste and serve immediately.

FRIDAY Tofu, Mushrooms and Greens in Teriyaki Sauce

IMPERIAL/METRIC		AMERICAN
2 tbs	soya sauce	2 tbs
2 tsp	wine vinegar	2 tsp
1 tbs	raw cane sugar	1 tbs
pinch	(dry) mustard powder	pinch
1 tsp	sesame oil	1 tsp
¼-inch piece	fresh ginger root	¼-inch piece
1 clove	garlic	1 clove
1	spring onion (scallion)	1
2 oz (55g)	mushrooms	1 cup
3–4 oz (85–115g)	outer lettuce leaves	3–4 oz (85–115g)
4–5 oz (115–170g)	tofu	½–⅔ cup
2½–3 oz (70–85g)	eggless noodles	2½–3 oz
2 tsp	vegetable oil	2 tsp

1 Put the soya sauce, vinegar, sugar, (dry) mustard powder and sesame oil in a
   large bowl. Peel and grate the ginger root, crush the garlic, and chop the
   spring onion (scallion) finely. Add these ingredients to the bowl.
2 Slice the mushrooms. Wash, dry on kitchen (paper) towels, and coarsely chop
   the lettuce leaves. Dice the tofu. Put these ingredients into the bowl, mix well
   with the sauce, and leave for a few minutes.
3 Cook the noodles according to the packet instructions and drain.
4 Heat the vegetable oil in a wok and turn the contents of the bowl into it. Cook
   over a high heat, stirring frequently, for 5–7 minutes, until some of the
   moisture has been driven out of the sauce.
5 Serve the tofu mixture over the noodles.

SATURDAY LUNCH *Herbed Bean Salad*

IMPERIAL/METRIC		AMERICAN
½ 420g can	haricot (navy)/cannellini (great northern) beans	½ 14 oz can
good handful	at least 4 different fresh summer herbs (e.g. mint, marjoram, parsley, chives), finely chopped	good handful
1 tbs	olive oil	1 tbs
2 tsp	lemon juice	2 tsp
	sea salt and freshly ground black pepper to taste	

1 Drain and rinse the beans.
2 Put the beans in a serving dish and mix in the herbs, olive oil, lemon juice, and seasoning to taste. Serve with wholemeal (whole wheat) bread.

Autumn/ Winter Recipes

Week 1

Shopping list

....

VEGETABLES AND FRUIT
1 small cauliflower
1 small potato
Parsley
4 small onions
1 small courgette (zucchini)
2 small carrots
1 small banana
1 lemon
10–12 oz (285–350g)
   tomatoes
Black olives
Garlic
Small chunk swede (rutabaga)
2 oz (55g) mushrooms
6–8 Brussels sprouts
Fresh ginger root
Frozen peas
Salad ingredients

MISCELLANEOUS
6 oz (170g) aduki beans
Sesame seeds
Broken cashews
Tabasco sauce
2 oz (55g) roasted peanuts
Gram (garbanzo bean) flour
Tahini

Check that you have all the staples listed on pages xiii and xiv.

SUNDAY LUNCH Cream of Cauliflower Soup

IMPERIAL/METRIC		AMERICAN
¼–⅓ small	cauliflower*	¼–⅓ small
1 small	potato	1 small
¼ pint (150ml)	water	⅔ cup
¼ pint (150ml)	soya milk	⅔ cup
½ tbs	vegan margarine	½ tbs
	sea salt, freshly ground black pepper and a little freshly grated nutmeg	
1 tbs	chopped parsley	1 tbs

1 Chop the cauliflower and potato (peeled if preferred, but it's not really necessary).
2 Put the vegetables into a saucepan with the water; bring to the boil, lower the heat, cover the pan, and simmer for about 15 minutes, until the potato is soft.
3 Empty the contents of the saucepan into a liquidizer, add the soya milk, and blend thoroughly.
4 Return to the saucepan and re-heat gently. Stir in the margarine and seasoning.
5 Serve immediately, sprinkled with parsley.

* The rest will be used later in the week (see pages 105 and 106).

SUNDAY DINNER. *Aduki Bean and Vegetable Crumble*

IMPERIAL/METRIC		AMERICAN
2 oz (55g)	aduki beans*	¼ cup
1 small	onion	1 small
1 tbs	oil	1 tbs
1 small	carrot	1 small
1 small	courgette (zucchini)	1 small
¼ tsp	sage	¼ tsp
2 tsp	soya sauce	2 tsp
1 oz (30g)	vegan margarine	⅛ cup
2 oz (55g)	wholemeal (whole wheat) flour	½ cup
1 tbs	sesame seeds	1 tbs
	sea salt and freshly ground black pepper to taste	

1 In the morning cover the beans with boiling water and leave to soak for several hours. Then drain the water, cover with lots of fresh cold water, bring to the boil, lower the heat and simmer for about 45 minutes until soft. Add a little sea salt only at the end of the cooking time.

2 Chop the onion and sauté it briefly in the oil in a saucepan. Dice the carrot and courgette (zucchini) and add them to the saucepan. Sauté for about 3–4 minutes.

3 Add the sage, soya sauce and drained beans to the saucepan and stir well. Remove from the heat and set aside.

4 Rub the margarine into the flour finely. Stir in the sesame seeds and seasoning to taste.

5 Put the bean mixture into a greased casserole or baking dish and cover with the crumble mixture. Bake at 400°F (200°C) Gas Mark 6 for about half an hour.

* If preparing the whole week's menus then soak and cook 6 oz (175g) ¼ cup beans; use a third of them for this dish and store the remainder (in the liquid they were cooked in) in the fridge until required.

SUNDAY DESSERT *Baked Banana Halves*

IMPERIAL/METRIC		AMERICAN
1 tsp	vegan margarine	1 tsp
1 small	banana	1 small
1 tsp	lemon juice	1 tsp
1 tbs	raw sugar	1 tbs
pinch	ground cinnamon	pinch
handful	cashew pieces	handful
	soya yogurt (optional)	

1 Heat the margarine in a baking dish in a 400°F (200°C) Gas Mark 6 oven for about 5 minutes.
2 Slice the banana in half lengthwise and turn the halves in the margarine so they are well coated.
3 Sprinkle the banana halves with lemon juice, sugar, cinnamon and cashew pieces. Bake in the oven for about 15 minutes.
4 Serve immediately, topped with soya yogurt if desired.

MONDAY *Spaghetti with Olive Sauce*

IMPERIAL/METRIC		AMERICAN
6 oz (170g)	very ripe tomatoes	6 oz
4–6	black olives	4–6
1 clove	garlic	1 clove
2 tbs	olive oil	2 tbs
¼ tsp	oregano	¼ tsp
	freshly ground black pepper	
1 tbs	chopped parsley	1 tbs
3 oz (85g)	wholemeal (whole wheat) spaghetti	3 oz

1 Pour boiling water over the tomatoes, leave for a minute, drain, run under cold water and skin.
2 Chop the tomatoes coarsely. Chop the olives finely. Crush the garlic.
3 Heat the oil in a saucepan. Add the tomatoes, olives, garlic, oregano and pepper. Simmer uncovered, over a low heat for about 15 minutes, stirring occasionally. Add the parsley and cook for 2 minutes longer.
4 Meanwhile, cook the spaghetti, and when it is ready drain it and pour the sauce over it. This is nice accompanied by a side salad.

TUESDAY *Vegetable Stew*

IMPERIAL/METRIC		AMERICAN
1 small	onion	1 small
small chunk	swede (rutabaga)	small chunk
1 small	carrot	1 small
2 oz (55g)	mushrooms	1 cup
6–8	Brussels sprouts	6–8
1 tbs	vegetable oil	1 tbs
few sprigs	cauliflower	few sprigs
1 tbs	tomato paste	1 tbs
½ tsp	marjoram	½ tsp
1	bay leaf	1
	freshly ground black pepper	
¼ pint (150ml)	water	⅔ cup
	soya sauce to taste	
as required	wholemeal (whole wheat) bread	as required

1 Chop the onion finely. Dice the swede (rutabaga) and carrot into roughly the same size pieces. Slice the mushrooms. Halve the sprouts.
2 Heat the oil in a saucepan and add the vegetables. Stir well for 2–3 minutes. Add the tomato paste, the herbs and the pepper, then pour in the water. Stir well, bring to the boil, lower the heat, cover the pan, and simmer for 15–20 minutes, by which time most or all of the water should have been absorbed and the vegetables should all be tender.
3 Stir in a little soya sauce to taste, and serve immediately, accompanied by thick slices of bread.

WEDNESDAY *Cauliflower and Pea Curry*

IMPERIAL/METRIC		AMERICAN
4–6 oz (100–150g)	cauliflower	4–6 oz
1 small	onion	1 small
1 tbs	vegan margarine	1 tbs
1 clove	garlic	1 clove
¼-inch piece	fresh ginger root	¼-inch
½ tsp	ground coriander	½ tsp
½ tsp	ground cumin	½ tsp
¼ tsp	garam masala	¼ tsp
¼ tsp	chilli powder	¼ tsp
(or more to taste)		(or more to taste)
1 tbs	tomato paste	1 tbs
4 tbs	water	4 tbs
	sea salt to taste	
2 oz (55g)	frozen peas	⅓ cup
1 tbs	soya milk	1 tbs
2½–3 oz (70–85g)	brown rice*	⅓–½ cup

1 Chop the cauliflower into florets and cook in a very small amount of water for about 5 minutes. Drain.

2 Grate the onion coarsely. Heat the margarine in a saucepan and add the onion. Cook briefly until it begins to change colour. Meanwhile, crush the garlic and grate or finely chop the ginger. Add them to the saucepan and stir well. Cook for another minute or so.

3 Stir in the spices and cook for about 30 seconds longer. Then add the tomato paste and water, plus a little salt if required. Bring to the boil, then stir in the cauliflower and peas. Lower the heat, cover the pan, and cook for about 5 minutes, until the cauliflower and peas are tender. Stir in the soya milk and serve the over rice, accompanied by mango chutney and a poppadum if desired.

* If preparing the week's menus then cook a double amount of rice and store half of it (after cooling) in the fridge.

T꜉ʜᴜʀꜱᴅᴀʏ *Aduki Beans, Rice and Tomatoes*

IMPERIAL/METRIC		AMERICAN
1 small	onion	1 small
1 clove	garlic	1 clove
1 tbs	oil	1 tbs
4–6 oz (150–170g)	tomatoes	4–6 oz
2 oz (55g)	aduki beans, cooked	¼ cup
2½–3 oz (70–85g)	brown rice, cooked	⅓–½ cup
2 tsp	soya sauce	2 tsp
½ tsp	cider vinegar	½ tsp
	black pepper to taste	
	few drops Tabasco sauce	

1 Chop the onion and garlic. Sauté in the oil in a saucepan until beginning to brown.
2 Skin and chop the tomatoes. Add them to the pan and cook for 2–3 minutes longer.
3 Add the drained beans and cooked rice to the pan and cook for a few minutes longer. Add the soya sauce, vinegar, pepper and Tabasco sauce and stir well before serving.

FRIDAY *Peanut Sausages*

IMPERIAL/METRIC		AMERICAN
2 oz (55g)	roasted peanuts*	⅓ cup
2 oz (55g)	wholemeal (whole wheat) breadcrumbs	2 oz
1 tbs	gram (garbanzo bean) flour	1 tbs
3 tsp	tomato paste	3 tsp
¼ tsp	marjoram	¼ tsp
1 tsp	soya sauce	1 tsp
4 tbs	water	¼ cup
	vegetable oil as required	
	salad ingredients	

1   Grind the peanuts. Put them in a bowl with the breadcrumbs, gram (garbanzo bean) flour, tomato paste, marjoram and soya sauce. Add the water and stir well.
2   Form the mixture into sausage shapes. Heat a little oil in a frying pan (skillet) and fry the sausages for 5–7 minutes, turning frequently. Serve with a side salad.

* The best kind of peanuts to use are the dry-roasted unsalted ones available at some wholefood shops. Second-best (only because they are so much more time-consuming) is to buy nuts in shells and shell them. If neither of those alternatives are possible then get roasted salted peanuts, rinse them as thoroughly as possible and dry them on kitchen paper.

SATURDAY LUNCH *Aduki Spread*

IMPERIAL/METRIC		AMERICAN
2 oz (55g)	aduki beans, cooked	¼ cup
½ tbs	oil	½ tbs
2 tsp	soya sauce	2 tsp
3 tsp	tahini	3 tsp
1 tbs	chopped parsley	1 tbs
	wholemeal (whole wheat) toast	

1 Drain the beans and put them in a bowl. Mash them lightly.
2 Heat the oil in a saucepan. Add the beans, soya sauce, tahini and parsley. Mix well and cook over a low heat for 5–7 minutes, stirring occasionally, by which time the mixture should have thickened.
3 Remove from the heat. Serve warm on toast.

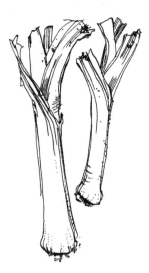

Week 2

Shopping list

VEGETABLES AND FRUIT

2 small leeks
4 small onions
6 oz (175g) mushrooms
1 cooking apple
3 small carrots
3 oz (85g) broccoli
9–10 oz (255–285g) potatoes
1 green pepper
4 oz (115g) tomatoes
Garlic
Frozen peas
⅛ cucumber
Lemon
Seasonal vegetables as desired
   (for Sunday dinner)

MISCELLANEOUS

8–12 oz (225–340g) firm
   tofu
Mustard
2 oz (55g) walnuts
1 oz (30g) sunflower seeds
Rolled oats
Maple syrup
Cashews
Semolina (farina)
7 oz (200g) can red kidney
   beans
Desiccated (shredded)
   coconut
6 oz (170g) wholemeal
   (whole wheat) macaroni
2 oz (55g) almonds
Roasted peanuts
Tabasco sauce

Check that you have all the staples listed on pages xiii and xiv.

SUNDAY LUNCH *Scrambled Tofu and Leek*

IMPERIAL/METRIC		AMERICAN
1 small	leek	1 small
3 tsp	vegan margarine	3 tsp
4–6 oz (115–170g)	firm tofu*	½–¾ cup
1 tsp	turmeric	1 tsp
2 tsp	soya sauce	2 tsp
2 tsp	mustard	2 tsp
	freshly ground black pepper	
as required	wholemeal (whole wheat) toast	as required

1 Wash and chop the leek finely. Heat the margarine in a saucepan and add the leek. Stir well, then cover the pan, and cook over a very low heat for about 5 minutes.
2 Mash the tofu in a small bowl with the turmeric, soya sauce, mustard and pepper to taste.
3 Add the tofu mixture to the saucepan and mix well. Cook until the tofu mixture is well heated and serve immediately over hot toast.

* If making the whole week's menus then slice the remaining 4–6 oz (115–170g)/½–¾ cup of the tofu into 2 or 3 pieces and place in the freezer until required.

Walnut and Mushroom Roast

IMPERIAL/METRIC		AMERICAN
1 small	onion	1 small
2 oz (55g)	mushrooms	1 cup
1 tbs	vegetable oil	1 tbs
1 oz (30g)	walnuts	¼ cup
1 oz (30g)	sunflower seeds	¼ cup
⅛ pint (65ml)	soya milk	⅓ cup
2 oz (55g)	wholemeal (whole wheat) breadcrumbs	1 cup
⅛ tsp	sage	⅛ tsp
¼ tsp	basil (sweet)	¼ tsp
	sea salt to taste	

1   Chop the onion and mushrooms finely. Sauté over a low heat in the oil for about 3 minutes, until tenderized.
2   Chop the walnuts coarsely. Grind the sunflower seeds finely.
3   Add all the rest of the ingredients to the onions and mushrooms, and mix well. Transfer to a greased baking dish and bake in a 350°F (180°C) Gas Mark 4 oven for about 45 minutes. Serve with Creamy Gravy (see recipe right) if desired and seasonal vegetables. (The water used in cooking the vegetables can be kept refrigerated for use as stock later in the week.)

Creamy Gravy

IMPERIAL/METRIC		AMERICAN
½ oz (15g)	rolled oats	⅛ cup
⅛ pint (65ml)	warm water	⅓ cup
1 tsp	vegetable oil	1 tsp
½ tsp	yeast extract	½ tsp
(or more to taste)		(or more to taste)

1 Put the oats, water and oil in a liquidizer and blend thoroughly.
2 Pour the mixture into a small saucepan and heat gently, stirring constantly until it has thickened. Stir in the yeast extract. If the mixture is too thick add a little more water. (N.B. This can be made earlier and reheated when serving the roast.)

SUNDAY DESSERT Baked Maple Apple Halves

IMPERIAL/METRIC

IMPERIAL/METRIC		AMERICAN
1	cooking (tart) apple	1
2 tsp	water	2 tsp
2 tbs	maple syrup	2 tbs
1 tsp	vegan margarine	1 tsp

1 Halve the apple cross-wise and core it.
2 Put the water in the bottom of a greased baking dish. Put the apple halves in the dish, cut side up. Pour a tbs of maple syrup over each half, and dot with the margarine.
3 Bake the apple halves in a 350°F (180°C) Gas Mark 4 oven for 40–45 minutes. If possible, baste the apple halves once or twice during this time. Serve hot.

MONDAY *Uppama (A South Indian Dish)*

IMPERIAL/METRIC		AMERICAN
1 small	onion	1 small
1 tbs	vegetable oil	1 tbs
1 tsp	mustard seeds	1 tsp
1 tbs	cashew pieces	1 tbs
1 tsp	ground coriander	1 tsp
½ tsp	ground cumin	½ tsp
1 tsp	turmeric	1 tsp
⅛–¼ tsp	chilli powder	⅛–¼ tsp
1 small	carrot	1 small
3 oz (85g)	broccoli florets	3 oz
1 tsp	raisins	1 tsp
½ pint (275ml)	water	1⅓ cups
	sea salt to taste	
3 oz (85g)	wholemeal (whole wheat) semolina (farina)	½ cup
1–2 tsp	vegan margarine	1–2 tsp

1. Chop the onion and sauté it in the oil in a saucepan for 2–3 minutes.
2. Add the mustard seeds and cashews and cook for a further 2 minutes.
3. Add the coriander, cumin, turmeric and chilli powder and cook for another minute.
4. Chop the carrot and broccoli quite finely. Add to the saucepan along with the raisins and stir well. Pour in the water, bring to the boil, lower the heat, cover the pan and cook for 3–4 minutes. Season to taste.
5. Pour in the semolina (farina) very slowly, stirring all the time. As soon as it is all in the pan and well thickened, serve it, with the margarine spread over the top so that it melts into the mixture.

TUESDAY *Irish Stew with Frozen Tofu**

IMPERIAL/METRIC		AMERICAN
4–6 oz (115–170g)	frozen tofu	½–¾ cup
1 small	onion	1 small
6 oz (170g)	potatoes	6 oz
1 small	carrot	1 small
½ tsp	yeast extract	½ tsp
¼ pint (140ml)	vegetable stock or water	⅔ cup
2 oz (55g) plus	wholemeal (whole wheat) flour	½ cup plus
2 tbs		2 tbs
pinch	sea salt	pinch
1 tsp	baking powder	1 tsp
½ oz (15g)	vegan margarine	⅛ cup
	soya milk as required	
1 tbs	soya sauce	1 tbs
1 tbs	water	1 tbs
1 tsp	cider vinegar	1 tsp
1 tbs	vegetable oil	1 tbs

* It must be admitted that this is rather more complicated than most of the weekday dishes featured in this book; however, it really doesn't take that long, and it is a wonderfully satisfying dish on a cold winter's night.

1   Pour boiling water over the tofu, cover if possible, and leave for 10–15 minutes.
2   Chop the onion. Dice the potatoes and carrot into small pieces. Add the yeast extract to the stock or water and bring to the boil in a saucepan. Add the onions and potatoes, lower the heat, and leave to simmer for 7–10 minutes. Add the carrots and cook for a further 4–5 minutes.
3   While the vegetables are cooking put the 2 oz (5g) ½ cup flour in a bowl and mix in the salt and baking powder. Cut in the margarine, then pour in enough soya milk (about 2 tbs) to make a soft dough. Divide the dough into 4 balls.
4   Put the soya sauce, water and vinegar into a small bowl. Drain the tofu and squeeze it gently to extract excess liquid. Cut it into small cubes. Put the cubes into the bowl with the soya sauce mixture and stir them around; the liquid should be absorbed rapidly by the tofu.
5   Spread the 2 tbs of flour on a plate and turn the tofu cubes in it. Heat the oil in a frying pan (skillet) and stir-fry the tofu cubes until lightly browned.
6   Add the tofu cubes to the vegetable mixture and turn into an oven dish. Flatten the dough balls and place them on top. Place in a 425°F (220°C) Gas Mark 7 oven for 15 minutes and serve immediately.

WEDNESDAY *Jambalaya*

IMPERIAL/METRIC		AMERICAN
7 oz (200g) can	red kidney beans	7 oz can
½	green pepper	½
1 tbs	vegetable oil	1 tbs
4 oz (115g)	tomatoes	¼ lb
1 oz (30g)	walnuts	¼ cup
1 oz (30g)	desiccated (shredded) coconut	⅓ cup
1 tsp	tomato paste	1 tsp
1 tbs	water	1 tbs
2½–3 oz (70–85g)	cooked brown rice*	¼–½ cup

1 Drain and rinse the beans.
2 Chop the pepper and sauté it in the heated oil in a saucepan for a minute or two.
3 Skin and chop the tomatoes. (The easiest way to skin tomatoes is to pour boiling water over them, and then leave them for a minute before draining them, after which the skin comes away easily – rinse them with cold water if they are too hot to handle.) Chop the walnuts coarsely.
4 Add the tomatoes, walnuts, coconut, tomato paste and water to the saucepan and stir well. Add the beans. Cover the pan and leave the mixture to simmer on a very low heat for about 10 minutes, stirring occasionally. Serve over the rice.

* If making the whole week's menus then cook 5–6 oz (150–170g)/1 cup rice, and store half of it in the fridge.

THURSDAY *Macaroni and Vegetable Stew*

IMPERIAL/METRIC		AMERICAN
3 oz (85g)	wholemeal (whole wheat) macaroni or other pasta shape*	3 oz
1 small	leek	1 small
1 small	carrot	1 small
1 small	potato	1 small
2 oz (55g)	mushrooms	2 oz
1 tbs	vegetable oil	1 tbs
1	bay leaf	1
⅛ pint (65ml)	water	⅓ cup
½ tsp	yeast extract	½ tsp

1 Cook the macaroni until tender and drain.
2 Meanwhile, dice the vegetables into small pieces. Heat the oil in a saucepan and stir-fry them for about 2 minutes. Add the bay leaf and the water, bring to the boil, lower the heat, cover the pan and simmer until the vegetables are tender, about 10–15 minutes.
3 Stir in the yeast extract, then add the macaroni and stir well. Cook for a couple of minutes longer, remove the bay leaf and serve.

* If making the whole week's menus then cook 6 oz (170g) 1½ cups macaroni and store half of it in a container in the fridge until Saturday.

FRIDAY *Stir-fried Vegetable Rice with Almonds*

IMPERIAL/METRIC		AMERICAN
2 oz (55g)	almonds	½ cup
1 small	onion	1 small
1 tbs	vegetable oil	1 tbs
1 clove	garlic	1 clove
½	green pepper	½
1 small	carrot	1 small
2 oz (55g)	mushrooms	2 oz
2 oz (55g)	frozen peas	2 oz
2–3 oz (55–85g)	brown rice, cooked	⅓–½ cup
3–4 tsp	soya sauce	3–4 tsp

1 Put the almonds under the grill (broiler) and toast until browned.
2 Chop the onion. Heat the oil in a frying pan (skillet) or wok and add the onion. Cook for a minute or two. Chop the garlic finely and add to the pan; sauté for 2–3 minutes longer.
3 Chop the green pepper and carrot finely. Slice the mushrooms. Add these to the pan along with the peas. Stir-fry the vegetables for 3–5 minutes.
4 Add the rice and soya sauce to the vegetables and stir well. Stir-fry for an additional 3–5 minutes.
5 Mix the almonds into the rice and serve immediately.

SATURDAY LUNCH *Macaroni Salad with an Indonesian Flavour*

IMPERIAL/METRIC		AMERICAN
3–4 oz (85–115g)	white cabbage	3–4 oz
⅛	cucumber	⅛
3 oz (85g)	wholemeal (whole wheat) macaroni (or other pasta shape) cooked, drained and cooled	3 oz
2–3 tsp	roasted peanuts	2–3 tsp
1 tbs	peanut butter	1 tbs
2 tbs	soya milk	2 tbs
1 tsp	soya sauce	1 tsp
1 tsp	lemon juice	1 tsp
⅛ tsp	garlic salt	⅛ tsp
¼ tsp	powdered ginger	¼ tsp
¼ tsp	raw sugar	¼ tsp
few drops	Tabasco sauce	few drops

1 Grate the cabbage coarsely. Dice the cucumber finely.
2 Place the macaroni, cabbage, cucumber and peanuts in a bowl.
3 Put the remainder of the ingredients into the liquidizer and blend well.
4 Pour the peanut butter dressing over the ingredients in the bowl and mix thoroughly before serving.

Week 3

Shopping list

VEGETABLES AND FRUIT
1 aubergine (eggplant)
7 small onions
10 oz (285g) mushrooms
Seasonal vegetables
  (for Sunday dinner)
1 pear
1 small potato (plus
  additional for Sunday
  and/or Thursday if desired)
1 small carrot
6 Brussels sprouts
Garlic
Fresh ginger root
5 small tomatoes
1 small green pepper
1 small red pepper

MISCELLANEOUS
½ lb (225g) tempeh
1 x 7 oz (200g) can sweetcorn
Tahini
Wholemeal (whole wheat)
  noodles
Mustard
Millet
Miso
1 x 15½ oz (440g) can chick
  peas (garbanzo beans)

Check that you have all the staples listed on pages xiii and xiv.

SUNDAY LUNCH Savoury Aubergine (Eggplant) on Toast

IMPERIAL/METRIC		AMERICAN
½ small	aubergine (eggplant)	½ small
1 small	onion	1 small
1 tbs	olive oil	1 tbs
	sea salt and freshly ground black pepper to taste	
	wholemeal (whole wheat) toast	

1 Put the halved aubergine (eggplant) cut side down on a baking dish (the remaining half should immediately be wrapped and refrigerated) and bake at 400°F (200°C) Gas Mark 6 for about half an hour, by which time it should be soft. Leave to cool.
2 Slice the onion thinly. Fry the sliced onion in the olive oil in a frying pan (skillet) until lightly browned.
3 Scrape the aubergine (eggplant) flesh from the skin and discard the skin. Chop the flesh coarsely. Add it to the frying pan (skillet), and continue cooking for a couple of minutes longer. Season to taste and serve immediately over hot toast.

Tempeh and Sweetcorn Roast with Tahini/ Mushroom Sauce

IMPERIAL/METRIC		AMERICAN
	Roast	
⅛ pint (65ml)	water*	⅓ cup
1 tbs	soya sauce*	1 tbs
4 oz (115g)	tempeh*	½ cup
1 small	onion	1 small
1 tbs	vegetable oil	1 tbs
½ x 7 oz (200g) can	sweetcorn	½ cup
1 oz (30g)	fresh wholemeal (whole wheat) breadcrumbs	½ cup
1 tbs	soya milk	1 tbs
pinch	thyme	pinch
	sea salt and freshly ground black pepper to taste	
	Sauce	
2 oz (55g)	mushrooms	1 cup
2 tsp	vegetable oil	2 tsp
2 tbs	water	2 tbs
1 tbs	tahini	1 tbs
2 tsp	soya sauce	2 tsp
	seasonal vegetables as desired**	

* If making the whole week's menus, use double these ingredients; follow instruction 1 for the whole square of tempeh, then cool it and refrigerate until required later in the week.
** If boiling potatoes, an extra 6–8 oz (170–225g) may be cooked, cooled and refrigerated for use later in the week.

1 Bring the water and soya sauce to the boil in a small pan, place tempeh
   (defrosted if frozen) in it, lower the heat, cover the pan and simmer for 10
   minutes; turn the tempeh over and simmer for a further 10 minutes. Drain.
2 Chop the onion. Sauté in the oil in a saucepan for 3–4 minutes until softened.
   Remove from the heat. Mash the tempeh into the pan, then add the drained
   corn, breadcrumbs, milk, thyme and seasoning; mix well. Turn into an oiled
   oven dish and bake at 305°F (180°C) Gas Mark 4 for about half an hour.
3 To make the sauce, chop the mushrooms and sauté them in the oil in a small
   pan until tender. Stir in the water, tahini, and soya sauce. Bring to the boil,
   stirring, then lower the heat and simmer for a couple of minutes. Serve the
   roast with the sauce poured over it, accompanied with seasonal vegetables.

Baked Pear

IMPERIAL/METRIC		AMERICAN
1	pear (preferably just ripe)	1
as required	raw sugar and vegan margarine	as required
pinch	powdered ginger	pinch

1 Peel the pear and slice it into slivers. Place in an oiled baking dish.
2 Sprinkle a little raw sugar over the top and add a few flakes of margarine and a pinch of ginger.
3 Bake at 350°F (180°C) Gas Mark 4 for 20–30 minutes.

MONDAY *Noodles with Creamy Leek and Mushroom Sauce*

IMPERIAL/METRIC		AMERICAN
3–3½ oz (85–100g)	wholemeal (whole wheat) noodles	3–3½ oz
1 small	leek	1 small
1½ tbs	vegan margarine	1½ tbs
4 oz (115g)	mushrooms	2 cups
1½ tbs	wholemeal (whole wheat) flour	1½ tbs
⅛ pint (70ml)	soya milk	⅓ cup
½ tsp	mustard	½ tsp
½ tsp	marjoram	½ tsp
	sea salt and freshly ground black pepper to taste	

1. Cook the noodles until tender in boiling salted water.
2. Clean and chop the leek finely. Melt 1 tbs of the margarine in a saucepan and sauté the chopped leek for 3–4 minutes.
3. Slice the mushrooms and add them to the pan; cook for a further 3–4 minutes.
4. Stir the flour into the pan, then slowly add the milk, stirring constantly (if a thinner sauce is desired add a little more than specified) until thickened and boiling. Lower the heat and simmer while adding mustard, marjoram and seasoning.
5. When the noodles are cooked, drain them and toss them with the remaining ½ tbs margarine. Pour the sauce over them.

TUESDAY *Millet and Vegetable Stew*

IMPERIAL/METRIC		AMERICAN
2½–3 oz (70–85 g)	millet	½ cup
as required	water	as required
pinch	sea salt	pinch
1 small	onion	1 small
1 tbs	vegetable oil	1 tbs
1 small	potato	1 small
1 small	carrot	1 small
6	Brussels sprouts	6
1 tsp	miso	1 tsp
½ tsp	sage	½ tsp

1 Cover the millet with approximately 3 times its quantity in water (the exact amount really does not matter; you can always add a little extra at the end if necessary); add a pinch of salt. Cover, bring to the boil, then lower the heat and simmer until the water is absorbed and the millet is tender (20–30 minutes).

2 Meanwhile, chop the onion and sauté it in the oil in a frying pan (skillet) or wok for 2–3 minutes. Dice the potato finely and add it to the pan; stir-fry for 3–4 minutes longer. Add 2 tbs of water to the pan, cover it, and leave it to simmer over a gentle heat for 5–7 minutes, checking to make sure the water does not dry out (add a little more if necessary).

3 Dice the carrot finely. Chop the Brussels sprouts. Add them to the pan along with another tbs of water. Cook – covered – for about 5 minutes longer, or until the vegetables are crisp-tender.

4 When the millet is cooked remove it from the heat and stir in the miso and sage immediately. Then add the vegetables and mix in thoroughly.

WEDNESDAY *Curried Chick Peas (Garbanzo Beans)*

IMPERIAL/METRIC		AMERICAN
2½–3 oz (70–85g)	brown rice**	½ cup
1 small	onion*	1 small
1 tbs	vegetable oil*	1 tbs
1 small clove	garlic*	1 small clove
¼-inch piece	fresh ginger root*	¼-inch piece
1 small	tomato*	1 small
1 tsp	ground cumin*	1 tsp
1 tsp	ground coriander*	1 tsp
½ tsp	turmeric*	½ tsp
⅛–¼ tsp	chilli powder*	⅛–¼ tsp
	sea salt and freshly ground black pepper to taste*	
½ x 15½ oz (440g) can	chick peas (garbanzo beans)*	½ x 15½ oz can
⅛ pint (140ml)	water*	⅓ cup
1	bay leaf*	1

1 Set the rice on to cook. Chop the onion and sauté it for 2–3 minutes in the oil in a saucepan.
2 Crush the garlic. Peel and grate the ginger finely. Chop the tomato. Add these ingredients to the pan and cook for 2–3 minutes longer. Add the spices and seasoning to the pan and stir well.
3 Drain and rinse the chick peas (garbanzo beans). Add them to the pan along with the water and bay leaf. Bring to the boil, then lower the heat and simmer, uncovered, for about 10 minutes.
4 Remove the bay leaf and serve over the rice. This is nice with a poppadum or chapati and mango chutney.

* If making the whole week's menus then double all of these ingredients. Follow all of the instructions above, cool and then refrigerate half of the curry.
** If making the whole week's menus then cook double this amount of rice; cool and refrigerate half.

THURSDAY *Tempeh and Mushroom Stew on a Mashed Potato Base*

IMPERIAL/METRIC		AMERICAN
4 oz (115g)	tempeh	½ cup
1 small	onion	1 small
1 small clove	garlic	1 small clove
1 tbs	vegetable oil	1 tbs
4 oz (115g)	mushrooms	2 cups
1 small	tomato	1 small
1	bay leaf	1
1–2 tsp	soya sauce	1–2 tsp
6–8 oz (170–225g)	cooked potatoes	6–8 oz
	soya milk, vegan margarine and seasoning to taste	

1 Prepare the tempeh as described in the recipe for Sunday dinner (pages 124 and 125), or use tempeh previously prepared. Set aside.
2 Chop the onion and garlic and sauté in the oil for a minute or two. Slice the mushrooms, add them to the pan and cook for another minute or two.
3 Dice the tempeh. Cook the tomato. Add them to the pan, along with the bay leaf and soya sauce. Cook, uncovered, for about 5 minutes, stirring frequently.
4 Heat and mash the cooked potatoes with soya milk, margarine and seasoning to taste (or alternatively use a packet of vegan instant mashed potatoes). Make a mashed potato base, remove the bay leaf from the tempeh mixture, and pile it onto the base.

FRIDAY *Balkan Stew*

IMPERIAL/METRIC		AMERICAN
1 small	onion	1 small
1 small	green pepper	1 small
1 small	red pepper	1 small
1½ tbs	vegetable oil	1½ tbs
1 small clove	garlic	1 small clove
2 small	tomatoes	2 small
½ small	aubergine (eggplant)	½ small
	sea salt to taste	
pinch	cayenne pepper	pinch
3 tbs	water	3 tbs
2½–3 oz (70–85g)	brown rice, cooked	½ cup

1 Slice the onion and peppers thinly. Sauté them in the oil in a saucepan for about 3 minutes.
2 Crush the garlic. Chop the tomatoes. Dice the aubergine (eggplant). Add them to the pan and cook for a couple of minutes longer.
3 Add the seasoning and then the water. Bring to the boil, then lower the heat. Cover the pan and simmer for about 5 minutes.
4 Stir in the cooked rice and cook, covered, for about 5 minutes longer.

SATURDAY LUNCH Curried Chick Pea (Garbanzo Bean) and Sweetcorn Chowder

IMPERIAL/METRIC		AMERICAN
	curried chick peas (garbanzo beans) from Wednesday (page 129)	
3 tbs	soya milk	3 tbs
⅛ pint (70ml)	water	⅓ cup
½ x 7 oz (200g)	canned sweetcorn	about ½ cup

1 Put the curried chick peas (garbanzo beans) into the liquidizer along with the milk and water. Blend thoroughly.
2 Pour into a saucepan. Add the sweetcorn. Heat gently, stirring occasionally until nice and hot. (This makes a very thick soup; for a thinner one add more water or soya milk).

Week 4

Shopping list

VEGETABLES AND FRUIT
1 small carrot
9 oz (255g) mushrooms
Parsley
Lemon
Seasonal vegetables (for
  Sunday dinner)
5 small onions
Garlic
1 small green pepper
2 small tomatoes
1 small leek
4–6 oz (115–170g) cabbage

MISCELLANEOUS
Peanuts
4 oz (115g) dried chestnuts
10 oz (285g) packet tofu
Vanilla essence
Smokey Snaps (imitation
  bacon bits)
1 x 7 oz (200g) can tomatoes
1 x 15½ oz (440g) can
  haricot (navy) beans
Chinese noodles

Check that you have all the staples listed on pages xiii and xiv.

Carroty Bulgur Salad

IMPERIAL/METRIC		AMERICAN
1½ oz (45g)	bulgur wheat	¼ cup
1 small	carrot	1 small
1 oz (30g)	mushrooms	½ cup
1 tbs	chopped parsley	1 tbs
1 oz (30g)	peanuts	1¾ tbs
1 tbs	vegetable oil	1 tbs
1 tbs	lemon juice	1 tbs
pinch	mustard powder	pinch
	sea salt and freshly ground black pepper to taste	

1 Cover the bulgur wheat with cold water and leave it to soak for an hour or longer. Drain in a tea (dish) towel or muslin, and squeeze well to get rid of as much moisture as possible. Transfer to a bowl.

2 Grate the carrot coarsely. Slice the mushrooms. Add both to the bulgur, along with the parsley and peanuts, and mix well.

3 In a small cup mix the oil, lemon juice and mustard powder with a fork. Pour the mixture on the bulgur and mix thoroughly. Season to taste.

SUNDAY DINNER Savoury Chestnut Pudding

IMPERIAL/METRIC		AMERICAN
2 oz (55g)	dried chestnuts*	2 oz
¾ oz (20g)	vegan margarine	1½ tbs
2 oz (55g)	wholemeal (whole wheat) flour	½ cup
½ tsp	baking powder	½ tsp
¼ pint (140ml)	soya milk	⅔ cup
	sea salt and freshly ground	
	black pepper to taste	
	seasonal vegetables**	

1 Cover the chestnuts with boiling water and leave them to soak for several hours, then cook them until tender. (If the chestnuts are soaked in warm water in a wide rimmed thermos flask, or in a warm cupboard, they may be tender enough after soaking not to require more cooking).
2 Put the margarine in a baking dish and place in a hot oven to melt.
3 In a bowl mix the flour, baking powder, soya milk and seasoning, and add the melted margarine. Stir in the cooked drained chestnuts. Return the mixture to the baking dish and bake at 425°F (220°C) Gas Mark 7 for 20 minutes, then lower heat to 350°F (180°C) Gas mark 4 and continue cooking for a further 20 minutes. Serve with seasonal vegetables to taste.

*If making the whole week's menus then use double this amount of chestnuts; follow instruction 1, then cool and refrigerate half the chestnuts in their liquid.
**If making the whole week's menus then you could buy enough cabbage to use tonight and Friday.

Sweet Tofu 'Omelette'

IMPERIAL/METRIC		AMERICAN
4 oz (115g)	tofu	½ cup
1 tbs	soya milk	1 tbs
1 tbs	wholemeal (whole wheat) flour	1 tbs
¼ tsp	baking powder	¼ tsp
1 tbs	raw sugar	1 tbs
¼ tsp	vanilla essence	¼ tsp
	sugar-free or raw sugar jam	

1 Put half the tofu in a liquidizer with the soya milk and blend thoroughly.
2 Put the other half of the tofu in a small mixing bowl and mash. Add the flour, baking powder, sugar, vanilla, and the blended tofu. Mix well.
3 Spread the mixture thinly in a well-greased baking dish and bake at 350°F (180°C) Gas Mark 4 for 30–40 minutes.
4 With the help of a pancake turner carefully transfer the 'omelette' onto a serving dish. Spread jam to taste on top and eat while hot.

MONDAY *Spaghetti Ticino*

IMPERIAL/METRIC		AMERICAN
3 oz (85g)	wholemeal (whole wheat) spaghetti	½ cup
1 small	onion	1 small
1 small clove	garlic	1 small clove
1 small	green pepper	1 small
1 tbs	olive oil	1 tbs
2 oz (55g)	mushrooms	1 cup
1 tbs	wholemeal (whole wheat) flour	1 tbs
¼ pint (140ml)	soya milk	⅔ cup
	sea salt and freshly ground	
	black pepper to taste	
1 tsp	vegan margarine	1 tsp
1 tbs	nutritional yeast flakes or powder or	1 tbs
1 tsp	vegan Parmesan	1 tsp
2 tbs	Smokey Snaps (imitation bacon bits)	2 tbs

1 Cook the spaghetti until just tender.
2 Meanwhile, chop the onion, garlic and green pepper finely. Sauté them in the oil in a saucepan for 3–4 minutes. Slice the mushrooms; add them to the pan and sauté the mixture for a further 2 minutes.
3 Stir in the flour, then pour in the milk slowly, stirring constantly to avoid lumps. Bring to the boil, then lower the heat and simmer, uncovered, for a few minutes. Season to taste.
4 When the spaghetti is cooked, drain it and toss with the margarine and yeast or vegan Parmesan.
5 Remove the sauce from the heat and stir in the Smokey Snaps (imitation bacon bits). Pour the sauce over the spaghetti.

TUESDAY *Curried Tofu*

IMPERIAL/METRIC		AMERICAN
2–3 oz (55–85g)	brown rice*	½ cup
1 small	onion	1 small
1 tbs	vegan margarine	1 tbs
4–5 oz (115–140g)	tofu	½–⅔ cup
½ tsp	ground coriander	½ tsp
½ tsp	ground cumin	½ tsp
¼ tsp	turmeric	¼ tsp
⅛–¼ tsp	chilli powder	⅛–¼ tsp
½ tsp	garam masala	½ tsp
2 tbs	water	2 tbs
1 tbs	tomato paste	1 tbs
1 tbs	soya yogurt	1 tbs
	sea salt if required	

1 Cook the rice until tender.
2 Chop the onion. Sauté it in the margarine in a saucepan for about 3 minutes. Meanwhile, drain and dice the tofu.
3 Lower the heat and stir in the spices. Then add the tofu, stirring it well – but gently – so that it is well coated with the spices. After a minute or two add the water and stir in the tomato paste. Cover the pan and simmer for about 10 minutes. Stir in the yogurt, taste for seasoning and add salt if needed.
4 Serve the curry over the rice (accompanied by a chapati or poppadum and mango chutney if desired).

* If making the whole week's menus cook double this amount of rice; refrigerate half after it has cooled.

WEDNESDAY *Mediterranean Bean and Tomato Stew*

IMPERIAL/METRIC		AMERICAN
1 small	onion	1 small
1 small clove	garlic	1 small clove
1 tbs	olive oil	1 tbs
7 oz (200g) can	tomatoes	7 oz can
1	bay leaf	1
1 tbs	chopped parsley	1 tbs
1 tsp	oregano	1 tsp
½ x 15½ oz (440g) can	haricot (navy) beans	½ x 15½ oz can
as required	wholemeal (whole wheat) bread	as required

1 Slice the onion thinly. Crush the garlic. Sauté these ingredients in the olive oil in a saucepan for about 3 minutes.
2 Stir in the tomatoes, chopping them coarsely with the spoon while doing so. Add the bay leaf, parsley and oregano. Bring to the boil, then lower the heat, cover the pan and simmer for 7–10 minutes.
3 Drain the beans and add them to the pan. Cover the pan again and simmer for a further 4–7 minutes. Remove the bay leaf and serve accompanied with bread.

THURSDAY *Chestnut and Rice Savoury*

IMPERIAL/METRIC		AMERICAN
1 small	onion	1 small
1 tbs	vegetable oil	1 tbs
1 small	tomato	1 small
2 oz (55g)	mushrooms	1 cup
2½–3 oz (70–85g)	brown rice, cooked	½ cup
2 oz (55g)	dried chestnuts, soaked and cooked (see Sunday, page 135)	2 oz
2 tbs	water	2 tbs
1 tsp	yeast extract	1 tsp
1 tsp	tomato paste	1 tsp

1 Chop the onion and sauté it in the oil in a saucepan for about 3 minutes.
2 Skin and chop the tomato. Slice the mushrooms. Add them to the pan and cook for a further 3 minutes or so.
3 Add the rice and chestnuts to the pan and stir well. Then add the water, yeast extract and tomato paste. Mix together very thoroughly as it heats up so that the yeast extract is amalgamated evenly into the mixture. Continue cooking over a gentle heat until all the ingredients are well heated.

FRIDAY *Chow Mein*

IMPERIAL/METRIC		AMERICAN
3 oz (85g)	Chinese noodles	3 oz
1 small	leek	1 small
1 small clove	garlic	1 small clove
1 tbs	vegetable oil	1 tbs
4–6 oz (115–170g)	cabbage	4–6 oz
4 oz (115g)	mushrooms	2 cups
1 tbs	water	1 tbs
1 tbs	soya sauce	1 tbs
	freshly ground black pepper	

1   Cook the noodles according to the directions on the packet; drain and rinse with cold water.
2   Chop the leek finely. Crush the garlic. Heat the oil in a wok or frying pan (skillet) and stir-fry the leek and garlic for a minute or two.
3   Shred the cabbage. Slice the mushrooms. Add these ingredients to the wok and stir-fry them for a minute or two longer. Add the water and soya sauce, lower the heat, cover the wok, and leave to cook for a couple of minutes.
4   Uncover the wok, raise the heat, add the cooked noodles and lots of black pepper, and stir-fry for a couple of minutes longer before dishing up.

SATURDAY LUNCH *Beany Spread*

IMPERIAL/METRIC		AMERICAN
1 small	onion	1 small
1 tbs	vegan margarine	1 tbs
1 small	tomato	1 small
½ x 15½ oz (440g) can	haricot (navy) beans	½ x 15½ oz can
	sea salt and freshly ground black pepper to taste	

1 Chop the onion finely. Melt the margarine in a saucepan and sauté the onion for about 3 minutes.
2 Chop the tomato and add it to the pan. Cook for a further 2–3 minutes.
3 Drain the beans and put them into a bowl. Mash them coarsely (a potato masher or pastry blender is useful for this), leaving some of the beans whole.
4 Add the beans to the saucepan, stirring well. Season to taste, cook for a minute or two, then remove from the heat. Turn into a shallow bowl, leave to cool then chill in refrigerator. Spread on toast, crispbread, or in sandwiches.

Week 5

Shopping list

VEGETABLES AND FRUIT
9 small onions
Parsley
Seasonal vegetables (for
    Sunday dinner)
2 oz (55g) mushrooms
1 small banana
Lettuce
Other salad ingredients
1 small carrot
Garlic
6–7 oz (170–200g) potatoes

MISCELLANEOUS
15½ oz (440g) can tomatoes
2 oz (55g) walnuts
2 oz (55g) ground almonds
Miso
Brown rice flour
Chocolate, banana or
    strawberry-flavoured
    soya milk
Millet
15½ oz (440g) can borlotti
    (pinto) beans
Rolled oats
Soya flour
Baking powder
1 oz (30g) 1¾ tbs cashews
Smokey Snaps (imitation
    bacon bits)
Soya mayonnaise
Mango chutney
1 oz (30g) 1¾ tbs peanuts

Check that you have all the staples listed on pages xiii and xiv.

SUNDAY LUNCH *Tomato Soup*

IMPERIAL/METRIC		AMERICAN
1 small	onion*	1 small
1 tbs	vegetable oil*	1 tbs
7 oz (200g) can	tomatoes*	7 oz can
½ tsp	yeast extract*	½ tsp
½ tsp	marjoram*	½ tsp
½ tsp	basil (sweet)*	½ tsp
¼ pint (140ml)	water*	⅔ cup
	sea salt and freshly ground black pepper to taste	
1 tbs	chopped parsley	1 tbs

1 Chop the onion. Sauté in the oil for about 3 minutes.
2 Add the tomatoes, chopping them with a spoon while doing so. Add the yeast extract and herbs, bring to the boil, then lower the heat and simmer, uncovered, for about 10 minutes.
3 Put the water and about half the soup mixture into a liquidizer and blend thoroughly. Return to the saucepan, add the seasoning, bring to the boil, then simmer for another minute or two.
4 Serve topped with chopped parsley.

*If making the whole week's menus, use a large can of tomatoes and double all the starred ingredients; cool the half of the soup not eaten and then refrigerate for later use.

SUNDAY DINNER *Savoury Nut Pudding*

IMPERIAL/METRIC		AMERICAN
1 small	onion*	1 small
1 tbs	vegetable oil*	1 tbs
1 tbs	wholemeal (whole wheat) flour*	1 tbs
⅛ pint (70ml)	water*	⅓ cup
1 oz (30g)	walnuts*	¼ cup
1 oz (30g)	ground almonds*	¼ cup
1 oz (30g)	fresh wholemeal (whole wheat) breadcrumbs	½ cup
½ tsp	sage*	½ tsp
½ tsp	marjoram*	½ tsp
¼ tsp	thyme*	¼ tsp
1 tbs	soya sauce*	1 tbs
	sea salt and freshly ground black pepper to taste*	
	seasonal vegetables	

1 Chop the onion and sauté in the oil in a pan for about 3 minutes. Stir in the flour and then the water, heating until it thickens and boils. Remove the pan from the heat.
2 Grind the walnuts. Add them to the pan, as well as the ground almonds, breadcrumbs, herbs, soya sauce and seasoning. Mix well.
3 Turn the mixture into a pudding basin, cover with foil, and place in a large pan of simmering water; cover the pan, and steam the dish for about 1½ hours. Serve with cooked seasonal vegetables and with Mushroom-miso Gravy (see page 146).

*If making the whole week's menus double all of these ingredients and make double the quantity of the dish; cool and then refrigerate half.

Mushroom-miso Gravy

IMPERIAL/METRIC		AMERICAN
1 oz (30g)	mushrooms	½ cup
2 tsp	vegetable oil	2 tsp
⅛ pint (70ml)	warm water	⅓ cup
1 tsp	miso	1 tsp
½ tbs	brown rice flour	½ tbs

1 Chop the mushrooms. Sauté them in a small saucepan in the oil until tender.
2 Put the warm water, miso and rice flour into a liquidizer. Blend thoroughly.
3 Pour the mixture onto the mushrooms and stir well, over a low heat, until the gravy thickens.

SUNDAY DESSERT Delicious Blancmange

IMPERIAL/METRIC		AMERICAN
¼ pint (140ml) plus	chocolate, banana or strawberry-	⅔ cup plus
2 tbs	flavoured soya milk	2 tbs
3 tsp	cornflour (cornstarch)	3 tsp
	raw cane sugar, to taste	

1 Heat the ¼ pint (140ml) ⅔ cup milk in a saucepan. Meanwhile, mix the remaining 2 tbs milk with the cornflour (cornstarch) and a little sugar. When the milk is boiling pour it onto the cornflour (cornstarch) mixture, stir, then return the mixture to the saucepan, bring to the boil, stirring constantly, and boil for a minute or so.

2 Taste the thickened milk and stir in more sugar if required. Pour it into a dessert bowl and leave to cool, then refrigerate until ready to use.

MONDAY *Millet Chilli*

IMPERIAL/METRIC		AMERICAN
2 oz (55g)	millet*	½ cup
6 fl oz (170ml)	water	¾ cup
pinch	sea salt	pinch
1 small	onion	1 small
1 tbs	vegetable oil	1 tbs
1 tsp	ground cumin	1 tsp
1 tsp	oregano	1 tsp
½ tsp	garlic salt	½ tsp
¼–⅛ tsp	chilli powder	¼–⅛ tsp
½ x 15½ oz (440g) can	borlotti (pinto) beans	½ x 15½ oz can
⅛ pint (70ml)	water	⅓ cup
1 tbs	tomato paste	1 tbs

1 Cover the millet with the water and a pinch of salt. Bring to the boil, then lower the heat, cover and simmer for about 20 minutes, by which time the water should be absorbed and the millet tender.
2 Meanwhile, chop the onion and sauté it in the oil for about 3 minutes. Lower the heat and add the cumin, oregano, garlic salt and chilli powder. Stir well for a minute or so.
3 Drain and rinse the beans. Add them to the saucepan and stir for a minute or so longer. Add the water and the tomato paste. Raise the heat, bring to the boil, then lower the heat and simmer uncovered for about 5 minutes.
4 Add the cooked millet to the beans, stir well, and cook for a minute or two longer.

* If making the whole week's menus cook double this amount of millet in double the amount of water; cool and then refrigerate half.

TUESDAY *Nut Rissoles with Tomato Sauce*

IMPERIAL/METRIC		AMERICAN
	Rissoles	
	Savoury Nut Pudding from	
	Sunday (page 145)	
2 tbs	wholemeal (whole wheat) flour	2 tbs
2 tbs	rolled oats·	2 tbs
as required	vegetable oil	as required
	salad ingredients	
	Tomato Sauce*	
	Tomato Soup from Sunday	
	(page 144)	
½ oz (15g)	brown rice flour	⅛ cup
1 tbs	tomato paste	1 tbs

1 Mash the nut mixture in a bowl. Stir in the flour.
2 Spread the oats out on a plate. Form the nut mixture into 3 rissoles, and coat them well on both sides with the oats.
3 Heat a little oil in a frying pan (skillet) and fry the rissoles, turning them once, until nicely browned on both sides. Serve accompanied with a side salad and topped with tomato sauce.
4 To make the tomato sauce, pour the soup into a liquidizer and add the rice flour and tomato paste. Blend thoroughly. Pour into a saucepan, and heat gently until it thickens and comes to the boil. Simmer for a couple of minutes. (If you have not made the whole week's menus a good store-bought wholefood tomato sauce could be used instead).

* N.B. This will be twice as much as required for one meal; after letting the sauce cool, refrigerate half to be used on Thursday night.

WEDNESDAY *Vegetable Dumplings*

IMPERIAL/METRIC		AMERICAN
2½–3 oz (70–85g)	wholemeal (whole wheat) bread	2½–3 oz
¼ pint (140ml)	soya milk	⅔ cup
1 small	onion	1 small
1½ tbs	vegan margarine	1½ tbs
1 small	carrot	1 small
1 oz (30g)	mushrooms	½ cup
3 tbs	wholemeal (whole wheat) flour	3 tbs
2 tbs	soya flour	2 tbs
¼ tsp	baking powder	¼ tsp
	sea salt and freshly ground black pepper to taste	
good grate of	nutmeg	good grate of
1–2 tbs	nutritional yeast flakes or powder, or	1–2 tbs
1 tsp	vegan Parmesan	1 tsp

1 Dice the bread. Put the diced bread into a bowl and pour the milk over it. Turn over a few times then leave to soak.
2 Chop the onion finely. Sauté in a small saucepan in 1 tbs of the margarine for a minute or two. Chop the carrot and mushrooms finely. Add them to the pan and sauté for another minute or two. Lower the heat, cover the pan and leave the vegetables to cook in their own juices for 5–10 minutes.
3 Knead the milky bread well. Add both flours, baking powder, seasoning and nutmeg. Mix well. Stir in the vegetables. Leave to cool briefly.
4 Bring to the boil a largish saucepan of lightly salted water. Put tbs of the dumpling mixture into the water one at a time until all are in. Boil gently, uncovered, for 15–20 minutes.
5 Melt the remaining ½ tbs margarine.
6 Drain the dumplings carefully in a colander. Transfer them to a bowl or plate, pour the melted margarine over them and then sprinkle with the yeast or vegan Parmesan.

THURSDAY *Millet and Cashew Patties with Tomato Sauce*

IMPERIAL/METRIC		AMERICAN
1 small	onion	1 small
1 tbs plus additional for frying	vegetable oil	1 tbs plus additional for frying
2 oz (55g)	millet, cooked	½ cup
1 oz (30g)	cashews	¼ cup
2 tbs	nutritional yeast flakes or powder	2 tbs
	sea salt and freshly ground black pepper to taste	
	Tomato sauce (see Tuesday, page 149)	
	salad ingredients	

1   Chop the onion finely. Heat 1 tbs of the oil in a saucepan and sauté the onion for about 3 minutes.
2   Add the cooked millet to the pan and mash it well. Stir briefly, then remove from the heat.
3   Grind the cashews. Add them to the millet, along with the yeast and seasoning. Mix well and form into 4 patties.
4   Fry the patties in a little oil in a frying pan until lightly browned on both sides. Serve topped with the remainder of Tuesday's tomato sauce which has been gently reheated (or use a proprietary brand tomato sauce), accompanied with a side salad.

FRIDAY Pasta e Fagioli

IMPERIAL/METRIC		AMERICAN
6 oz (170g)	wholemeal (whole wheat) macaroni	6 oz
1 small	onion	1 small
1 small clove	garlic	1 small clove
1 tbs	olive oil	1 tbs
½ x 15½ oz (440g) can	borlotti (pinto) beans	½ x 15½ oz can
1 tbs	tomato paste	1 tbs
2 tbs	water	2 tbs
1 tsp	basil (sweet)	1 tsp
1 tbs	chopped parsley	1 tbs
	freshly ground black pepper	
1 tbs	Smokey Snaps (imitation bacon bits)	1 tbs

1 Cook the macaroni in boiling, lightly salted water until just tender.
2 Meanwhile, chop the onion and garlic finely. Sauté in the oil in a saucepan for about 3 minutes.
3 Add the beans, tomato paste, water and basil. Bring to the boil, then lower the heat and simmer, uncovered, for about 5 minutes.
4 Drain the macaroni and add it to the saucepan, along with the parsley, pepper to taste and Smokey Snaps (imitation bacon bits). Mix well and cook for a couple of minutes longer.

SATURDAY LUNCH *Curried Potato and Peanut Salad*

IMPERIAL/METRIC		AMERICAN
6–7 oz (170–200g)	potatoes	6–7 oz
1 small	onion	1 small
1 tbs	vegetable oil	1 tbs
¼ tsp	coriander	¼ tsp
¼ tsp	cumin	¼ tsp
¼ tsp	turmeric	¼ tsp
¼ tsp	powdered ginger	¼ tsp
pinch	chilli powder	pinch
2 tbs	soya mayonnaise	2 tbs
1 tbs	mango chutney	1 tbs
1 oz (30g)	peanuts	1¾ tbs
	sea salt and freshly ground black pepper to taste	
as required	lettuce	as required

1   Cook the potatoes until tender. Drain and cool.
2   Chop the onion. Sauté it in the oil in a small saucepan until beginning to brown. Lower the heat and add the spices; cook for a minute or so longer. Remove from the heat and cool.
3   Chop the potatoes and add them to the saucepan. Stir in the mayonnaise, chutney and peanuts, and season to taste. Transfer to a bowl, chill thoroughly and serve on a bed of lettuce.

Week 6

Shopping list

VEGETABLES AND FRUIT
Celery
Spring onions (scallions)
4 small onions
6 oz (170g) 3 cups mushrooms
Seasonal green vegetable
Potatoes
Mixed lettuce leaves
Lemon
Olives

MISCELLANEOUS
Tofu
Mustard
Golden syrup
Hard vegan cheese
Saffron
Salted peanuts
Cashews
400g (14 oz) can flageolet
    beans
400g (14 oz) can artichoke
    hearts
Flaked (slivered) almonds
Vegan mayonnaise
Kelp powder (optional)

Check that you have all the staples listed on pages xiii and xiv.

SUNDAY LUNCH *Creamy Celery Soup*

IMPERIAL/METRIC		AMERICAN
3 sticks	celery	3 sticks
2–3	spring onions (scallions)	2–3
2 tsp	vegan margarine	2 tsp
¼ pint (150ml)	water	⅔ cup
1 tbs	wholemeal (whole wheat) flour	1 tbs
¼ pint (150ml)	soya milk	⅔ cup
pinch	ground nutmeg	pinch
	sea salt and freshly ground black pepper to taste	

1 Chop the celery and spring onions (scallions) finely.
2 Melt the margarine in a saucepan, and sauté the vegetables for 2–3 minutes. Add the water, cover the pan, and bring to the boil. Lower the heat and leave to simmer for 15–20 minutes.
3 Mix the flour with a little of the milk, then add the rest. Stir this into the saucepan and bring to the boil, stirring frequently. Add nutmeg and seasoning to taste, lower the heat and simmer for a few more minutes before serving.

SUNDAY DINNER *Tofu Roast*

IMPERIAL/METRIC		AMERICAN
1 small	onion	1 small
2 oz (55g)	mushrooms	1 cup
1 tbs	vegetable oil	1 tbs
4–6 oz (115–170g)	tofu*	½–¾ cup
1½ oz (45g)	wholemeal (whole wheat) breadcrumbs	¾ cup
1 tbs	tomato paste	1 tbs
1 tbs	soya sauce	1 tbs
½ tsp	mustard	½ tsp
2 tbs	soya cream	2 tbs
1–2 tbs	water	1–2 tbs
	sea salt and freshly ground black pepper to taste	
as required	green vegetable and potatoes	as required

1 Chop the onion and mushrooms finely. Heat the oil in a frying pan (skillet), and sauté, for a few minutes, until tenderized.
2 Mash the tofu in a bowl. Add the breadcrumbs, tomato paste, soya sauce and mustard. Then add the onions and mushrooms and stir well. Mix in the cream, and then add just enough water to make a firm but cohesive mixture.
3 Transfer the mixture to a casserole dish, and either bake uncovered at 350°F (180°C) Gas Mark 4 for about 45 minutes until it is firm, or cover with greaseproof paper and microwave for 4 minutes; leave for a minute or two before turning out. Serve accompanied with seasonal vegetables.

* If making the whole week's menus, then refrigerate 3 oz (85g) ⅓ cup tofu, and freeze 2–3 oz (55–85g) ¼–⅓ cup tofu.

SUNDAY DESSERT *Fudge Custard*

IMPERIAL/METRIC		AMERICAN
½ oz (15g)	cornflour (cornstarch)	1 tbs
¼ pint (140ml)	soya milk	⅔ cup
1 tbs	vegan margarine	1 tbs
few drops	vanilla essence (extract)	few drops
2–3 tsp	golden syrup*	2–3 tsp
½ oz (15g)	vegan chocolate	½ oz

1 Mix the cornflour (cornstarch) with a little milk, then stir in the rest, transfer to a saucepan, add the margarine, and stir until thickened. Alternatively, if mixed in a microwave-safe measuring bowl this can be heated in the microwave instead, stirring every 30 seconds or so until thickened.
2 Remove from the heat and add the vanilla.
3 Spread the bottom of a small saucepan with a little margarine and heat the syrup until golden brown, taking care that it does not burn. Stir quickly into the white sauce.
4 Transfer the mixture to a small serving bowl; cool, then refrigerate.
5 Grate the chocolate and sprinkle it over the top before serving.

* I do not know if corn syrup, which is much thinner than golden syrup, would work in this recipe.

MONDAY *Spaghetti with Tofu-Peanut Sauce*

IMPERIAL/METRIC		AMERICAN
3 oz (85g)	wholemeal (whole wheat) spaghetti	3 oz
1 small	onion	1 small
2 tsp	vegetable oil	2 tsp
3 oz (85g)	tofu	⅓ cup
1 tbs	peanut butter	1 tbs
2 tsp	soya sauce	2 tsp
1–3 tbs	water	1–3 tbs
	sea salt and freshly ground black pepper to taste	
1 tbs	salted peanuts	1 tbs
	mixed salad ingredients	

1 Cook the spaghetti until just tender and drain.
2 Meanwhile, chop the onion finely and sauté in a small saucepan for a few minutes, stirring frequently, until just beginning to brown.
3 Put the tofu, peanut butter and soya sauce in a liquidizer. Add the onion and just enough water to make a thick sauce.
4 Return the liquidizer contents to the saucepan and heat gently; season to taste.
5 Serve over the spaghetti, topped with peanuts and accompanied with a side salad.

TUESDAY *Artichoke, Mushroom and Bean Gratin*

IMPERIAL/METRIC		AMERICAN
½ 14 oz (400g) can	flageolet beans	½ 14 oz can
½ 14 oz (400g) can	artichoke hearts	½ 14 oz can
1 oz (30g)	hard vegan cheese	⅛ cup
2 oz (55g)	mushrooms	1 cup
1 tbs	vegan margarine	1 tbs
1 tbs	wholemeal (whole wheat) flour	1 tbs
¼ pint (150ml)	soya milk	⅔ cup
	sea salt and freshly ground black pepper to taste	
1 oz (30g)	wholemeal (whole wheat) breadcrumbs	½ cup
as required	potatoes	as required

1 Drain and rinse the beans. Drain and rinse the artichoke hearts. Grate the cheese. Set aside.

2 Clean and slice the mushrooms. Melt the margarine in a saucepan and sauté the mushrooms for a few minutes until tender. Stir in the flour. Add the milk slowly, stirring constantly to avoid lumps, until thickened. Stir in the cheese, beans and artichoke hearts, and season to taste. Top with the breadcrumbs.

3 Brown the crumbs under a hot grill (broiler) and then microwave the gratin for 2 minutes. Alternatively bake in a fairly hot oven for about 15 minutes. Serve accompanied by boiled, roast or sautéed potatoes.

WEDNESDAY *Artichoke Paella*

IMPERIAL/METRIC		AMERICAN
2½ oz (70g)	brown rice	½ cup
1 small	onion	1 small
1 stick	celery	1 stick
1 tbs	olive oil	1 tbs
1 clove	garlic	1 clove
½ 14 oz (400g) can	artichoke hearts	½ 14 oz can
¼ pint (150ml)	water	⅔ cup
	sea salt and freshly ground black pepper to taste	
good pinch	saffron strands	good pinch
3–4	black olives	3–4
1–2 tsp	lemon juice	1–2 tsp
3 tbs	toasted flaked (slivered) almonds	3 tbs

1   In the morning cover the rice with boiling water and leave to soak. (This step may be omitted, but the rice will then take longer to cook and may need more water.)

2   Slice the onion and celery thinly. Heat the oil in a saucepan, and add the onion and celery. Crush the garlic and stir it into the pan. Sauté for about 3 minutes.

3   Drain and halve the artichoke hearts, and add them to the pan. Cook for a couple of minutes more, then add the drained rice and cook for a minute or two more.

4   Add the water and a little salt. Crush the saffron strands and add them to the pan, stirring well as the water comes to the boil to distribute it. Lower the heat, cover the pan, and cook until tender (15–20 minutes if rice has been pre-soaked).

5   Chop the olives finely.

6   When the rice has absorbed all the water and is tender, stir in the lemon juice. Taste for seasoning, add more salt if necessary, and pepper.

7   Transfer to a serving dish, and garnish with chopped olives and flaked (slivered) almonds.

THURSDAY *Celery and Cashew Timbale*

IMPERIAL/METRIC		AMERICAN
1 small	onion	1 small
1 tbs	vegan margarine	1 tbs
1	bay leaf	1
4 sticks	celery	4 sticks
2 oz (55g)	cashews	½ cup
1 tsp	wholemeal (whole wheat) flour	1 tsp
1 tbs	tomato paste	1 tbs
juice and rind of ¼	lemon	juice and rind of ¼
	grating of nutmeg	
	sea salt and freshly ground	
	black pepper to taste	
	boiled or roast potatoes	

1. Chop the onion. Heat the margarine in a saucepan, and add the onion and bay leaf. Cover the pan and cook over a very low heat for a few minutes until the onion is just tender but not brown.
2. Meanwhile, chop the celery coarsely, and steam or microwave in a little water until tender (it should have just a little 'bite' left). Drain, retaining the water.
3. Grind the cashews.
4. Uncover the saucepan and remove the bay leaf. Stir in the flour. Make the remaining celery water up to 3 fl oz (100ml/⅓ cup) and stir it in along with the tomato paste.
5. Add the celery, ground cashews, lemon juice and rind, nutmeg and seasoning. Stir well and heat thoroughly.
6. Serve with potatoes.

FRIDAY Yogurty Mushrooms and Beans on Bulgur Wheat

IMPERIAL/METRIC		AMERICAN
2 oz (55g)	bulgur wheat	⅓ cup
4 oz (115g)	mushrooms	2 cups
1 tbs	vegan margarine	1 tbs
½ 14 oz (400g) can	flageolet beans	½ 14 oz can
2 tbs	soya yogurt	2 tbs
1 tsp	wholemeal (whole wheat) flour	1 tsp
1 tsp	lemon juice	1 tsp
	grating of nutmeg	
	sea salt and freshly ground	
	black pepper to taste	

1 Cover the bulgur wheat with water, add a little salt, and cook until tender.
2 Meanwhile, clean and slice the mushrooms. Heat the margarine in a saucepan, and sauté the mushrooms for 3–4 minutes until just tender.
3 Drain and rinse the beans. Add them to the pan and heat thoroughly.
4 Put the yogurt into a small bowl, add the flour and mix well. Add this to the saucepan, and turn the heat down very low. When the mixture is hot add the lemon juice and seasoning to taste.
5 Serve the mushroom and bean mixtures over the bulgur wheat.

SATURDAY LUNCH *Tu-No Salad Sandwich*

IMPERIAL/METRIC		AMERICAN
2–3 oz (55–85g)	frozen tofu	¼–⅓ cup
1	spring onion (scallion)	1
1 small stick	celery	1 small stick
1 tbs	vegan mayonnaise	1 tbs
1 tsp	lemon juice	1 tsp
1 tsp	soya sauce	1 tsp
½ tsp	kelp powder (optional)	1 tsp
	lettuce leaves	
	wholemeal (whole wheat) toast	

1 Thaw the tofu by pouring hot water over it and leaving it for about 10 minutes. Drain and squeeze out all excess liquid. Crumble it into a bowl.
2 Chop the spring onion (scallion) and celery very finely. Add to the tofu. Stir in the mayonnaise, lemon juice, soya sauce, and kelp powder. Mix well. Serve on toast piled with lettuce leaves.

Week 7

Shopping list

VEGETABLES AND FRUIT

5 small onions
Garlic
2 small carrots
Celery
Small cauliflower
Small chunk swede (rutabaga)
3–4 oz (85–115g) Jerusalem
  artichokes
Parsley
Seasonal green vegetable
1 tomato
Small green pepper
Small chunk cucumber
1 small potato plus 6–8 oz
  (170–225g)

MISCELLANEOUS

15 oz (420g) can red kidney
  beans
Mexican chilli seasoning
Taco shells
Raisins
Custard powder
Frozen fishless fishcakes
Hard vegan cheese
Frozen peas
Tabasco sauce
Bacon-flavour soya bits
Cardamom
Chapatis

Check that you have all the staples listed on pages xiii and xiv.

SUNDAY LUNCH · *Tacos with Refried Beans*

IMPERIAL/METRIC		AMERICAN
1 small	onion	1 small
1 clove	garlic	1 clove
1 tbs	vegetable oil	1 tbs
1 7½ oz (210g) or ½ 15 oz (420g) can	red kidney beans	½ 15oz can
1–2 tsp	Mexican chilli seasoning	1–2 tsp
3	taco shells*	3

Optional extras:
shredded lettuce, grated vegan
hard cheese, vegan sour cream

1   Chop the onion. Crush the garlic. Heat the oil in a saucepan and sauté them until tenderized.
2   Drain the beans, retaining a little of the liquid in the can, and rinse them. Add them to the saucepan, along with a little of the liquid from the can and the chilli seasoning. Stir well for a minute or two, then mash the beans with a fork, potato masher, or pastry blender (they do not have to be particularly smooth). Continue cooking for a few minutes longer, stirring frequently.
3   Heat the taco shells. Divide the bean mixture between the 3 shells; top with optional extras and serve immediately.

---

* Taco shells generally come in packets of 12, which is a bit of a nuisance for single portions, but if immediately wrapped up again to keep out air they will keep for some time. (Another idea for using taco shells is shown in Week 9.)

SUNDAY DINNER *Vegetable Hotpot*

IMPERIAL/METRIC		AMERICAN
1 small	onion	1 small
1 tbs	vegetable oil	1 tbs
1 small	carrot	1 small
1 stick	celery	1 stick
¼ small	cauliflower	¼ small
small chunk	swede (rutabaga)	small chunk
3–4 oz (85–115g)	Jerusalem artichokes	3–4 oz
1 small	potato	1 small
¼ tsp	yeast extract	¼ tsp
¼ pint (150ml)	hot stock or water	⅔ cup
2 tbs	tomato paste	2 tbs
	black pepper to taste	
	crusty wholewheat bread	

1 Slice the onion thinly. Put the oil and onion in a small casserole dish, cover with greaseproof (waxed) paper, and microwave for 1 minute. (Alternatively, heat the oil in a large saucepan, and sauté the onion until tenderized.)
2 Peel and chop the other vegetables and put them in the casserole (or saucepan), mixing with the onion.
3 Dissolve the yeast extract in the stock or water and stir in the tomato paste. Pour this over the vegetables in the casserole. Cover with greaseproof paper, and microwave for 9 minutes, stirring the vegetables once or twice during that time. (Alternatively, mix in the saucepan, and transfer to the casserole. Bake, covered, in a slow oven for 2–3 hours, or in a hot oven for about an hour.)
4 Leave to stand for a minute, season and serve with crusty bread.

SUNDAY DESSERT *Bread and 'Butter' Pudding*

IMPERIAL/METRIC		AMERICAN
2 small slices	bread	2 small slices
as required	vegan margarine	as required
2 tbs	raisins	2 tbs
½ tbs	custard powder*	½ tbs
2 tsp	brown sugar	2 tsp
(or to taste)		(or to taste)
¼ pint (150ml)	soya milk	⅔ cup
grating	nutmeg	grating

1   Trim the crusts off the bread. Spread margarine on them and slice them into strips. Put one layer on the bottom of a small dish, cover with raisins and then another layer of bread.
2   Mix the custard powder and sugar with a little of the milk, then add the rest and stir well. Pour this over the bread and leave to soak up the custard for about 20 minutes.
3   Grate a little nutmeg over the top, cover the dish and microwave for 2½ minutes. Leave to stand for 30 seconds. Serve hot. (Alternatively, bake, uncovered, for about half an hour at 350°F (180°C) Gas Mark 4.)

* Americans should be able to find this in shops selling British foods. Alternatively, use the same amount of cornstarch and add a few drops of vanilla extract.

MONDAY *Fishless Fish Pie*

IMPERIAL/METRIC		AMERICAN
2	frozen fishless fishcakes	2
1 tbs	vegan margarine	1 tbs
1 tbs	wholemeal (whole wheat) flour	1 tbs
3½–4 fl oz (100–115ml)	soya milk	⅓–½ cup
1 oz	hard vegan cheese	¼ cup
	sea salt and freshly ground black pepper to taste	
1 tbs	chopped parsley	1 tbs
6–8 oz (170–225g)	mashed potato	6–8 oz
	seasonal green vegetable	

1 Grill (broil) the 'fishcakes' according to instructions.
2 Meanwhile, melt the margarine in a saucepan and stir in the flour. Slowly add the milk, stirring constantly to avoid lumps. Remove from the heat. Grate the hard vegan cheese and add it to the pan along with seasoning to taste and the parsley. Transfer to a greased oven dish.
3 Spread the mashed potato over the top.
4 Bake at 375°F (190°C) Gas Mark 5 for about 20 minutes or microwave for about 5 minutes.
5 Serve with a cooked green vegetable.

TUESDAY *Spaghetti with Cauliflower Romagna Style*

IMPERIAL/METRIC		AMERICAN
¼ small	cauliflower	¼ small
2 tsp	olive oil	2 tsp
1 tsp	vegan margarine	1 tsp
1 clove	garlic	1 clove
3 oz (85g)	wholemeal (whole wheat) spaghetti	3 oz
1 tbs	tomato paste	1 tbs
3 tbs	water	3 tbs
grinding	black pepper	grinding
as required	vegan Parmesan cheese	as required

1 Chop the cauliflower finely; wash and set aside.
2 Heat the oil and margarine in a saucepan. Crush the garlic, add it to the pan, and stir for a minute or two.
3 Add the cauliflower and cook for another minute or two. Put the spaghetti on to cook in a different saucepan.
4 Add the tomato paste, water and pepper to the cauliflower, and stir well. Bring to the boil, cover the pan and lower the heat. Leave to simmer for about 10 minutes.
5 Drain the spaghetti and transfer to a serving dish. Pour the cauliflower mixture over the spaghetti and sprinkle with lots of vegan Parmesan.

WEDNESDAY *Louisiana Red Beans and Rice*

IMPERIAL/METRIC		AMERICAN
2½–3 oz (70–85g)	brown rice	½ cup
1 small	onion	1 small
½ small	green pepper	½ small
1 stick	celery	1 stick
1 clove	garlic	1 clove
1 tbs	vegetable oil	1 tbs
1	tomato	1
1	bay leaf	1
¼ tsp	ground cumin	¼ tsp
¼ tsp	thyme	¼ tsp
1 tsp	wine vinegar	1 tsp
7½ oz (210g) or ½ 15 oz (420g) can	red kidney beans	½ 15 oz can
few drops	Tabasco sauce	few drops
2 tbs	bacon-flavour soya bits	2 tbs

1 Put the rice on to cook.
2 Chop the onion, green pepper, and celery; crush the garlic. Heat the oil in a saucepan, and sauté the vegetables for 3–4 minutes.
3 Skin the tomato and chop it. Add it to the pan with the bay leaf, cumin, thyme, vinegar and 1–2 tbs water (depending on the size and juiciness of the tomato). Simmer for 4–5 minutes longer.
4 Drain and rinse the beans. Add them to the pan, and sprinkle in the Tabasco sauce. Cook for 2–3 minutes longer.
5 Remove the bay leaf, stir in the bacon-flavour soya bits, and serve immediately over the rice.

THURSDAY *Cauliflower Pilau*

IMPERIAL/METRIC		AMERICAN
2½–3 oz (70–85g)	brown rice	½ cup
¼ small	cauliflower	¼ small
1 tbs	vegan margarine	1 tbs
1 small	onion	1 small
1 clove	garlic	1 clove
2 whole	cardamoms	2 whole
2	cloves	2
½ tsp	grated fresh ginger root	½ tsp
small	green chilli (optional)	small
½ tsp	garam masala	½ tsp
½ tsp	cinnamon	½ tsp
½ tsp	cumin seeds	½ tsp
	sea salt and freshly ground	
	black pepper to taste	
2 oz (55g)	soya yogurt	¼ cup
8 fl oz (225ml)	water	cup
	poppadum or chapati	

1   In the morning pour boiling water over the rice, cover and leave to soak.
2   In the evening drain and rinse the rice.
3   Chop the cauliflower into florets and wash.
4   Heat the margarine in a saucepan, and sauté the cauliflower until it is beginning to turn golden. Remove from the saucepan.
5   Chop the onion and garlic finely. Sauté in the margarine for 2–3 minutes, then add the cardamoms, cloves, and the rice. Stir-fry for a couple of minutes longer.
6   Chop the chilli finely (if using). Add it to the pan, along with the ginger, garam masala, cinnamon, cumin seeds and seasoning. Fry for a couple of minutes longer, then add the yogurt and water. Bring to the boil, cover the pan, lower the heat and simmer until the rice is tender and the liquid absorbed.
7   Serve accompanied by a poppadum or chapati.

FRIDAY Sweet and Sour Fish-cakes' and Vegetables

IMPERIAL/METRIC		AMERICAN
2½–3 oz (70–85g)	brown rice	½ cup
1 tsp	cornflour (cornstarch)	1 tsp
3 tbs	water	3 tbs
2 tsp	tomato ketchup	2 tsp
1 tsp	raw sugar	1 tsp
2 tsp	wine vinegar	2 tsp
2 tsp	soya sauce	2 tsp
2	frozen fishless fishcakes	2
1 small	onion	1 small
1 clove	garlic	1 clove
1 small	carrot	1 small
½ small	green pepper	½ small
small chunk	cucumber	small chunk
1 tbs	vegetable oil	1 tbs

1 Put the rice on to cook.
2 In a small bowl mix the cornflour (cornstarch) into the water. Add the ketchup, sugar, vinegar and soya sauce. Set aside.
3 Grill (broil) the 'fishcakes' according to instructions.
4 Chop the onion and garlic finely. Cut the carrot and green pepper into thin slivers. Peel and dice the cucumber.
5 Heat the oil in a wok and add the vegetables. Stir-fry them for about 3 minutes. Add the sauce mixture, mix well and simmer for a minute or so longer.
6 Dice the cooked 'fishcakes' and mix them in.
7 Serve immediately over the rice.

SATURDAY LUNCH *Indian Yogurt with Cauliflower and Peas*

IMPERIAL/METRIC		AMERICAN
¼ small	cauliflower	¼ small
1 oz (30g)	frozen peas	1 oz
½ tsp	cumin seeds	½ tsp
pinch	chilli powder or cayenne pepper	pinch
4 oz (115g)	soya yogurt	½ cup
	sea salt to taste	
	chapatis	

1 Cook the cauliflower and peas briefly until both are just tender (steamed or in a microwave). Drain, pour cold water over them, and leave them to drain further.
2 Meanwhile, put the cumin seeds under a hot grill (broiler) until they are lightly roasted. Remove from heat and grind.
3 Put the yogurt in a bowl. Add the vegetables, ground cumin, and seasonings. Mix well, cover and refrigerate for an hour or more.
4 Heat the chapatis. Tear off portions and stuff with the cauliflower mixture.

Week 8

Shopping list

VEGETABLES AND FRUIT

Spring onions (scallions)
3 onions
Garlic
4 oz (115g) mushrooms
1 banana
3 small fresh chillies
Fresh ginger root
Salad ingredients
Lemon
1 potato (about 6 oz/170g)

MISCELLANEOUS

Tofu
Vegan cream cheese
Bacon-flavour soya bits
Split red lentils
Vegan hard cheese
14 oz (420g) can coconut
 milk
7 oz (200g) can chopped
 tomatoes
15 oz (420g) can black-eyed
 beans (peas)
Couscous or bulgur wheat
Thin eggless noodles
Curry powder
Frozen peas
Chutney

Check that you have all the staples listed on pages xiii and xiv.

SUNDAY LUNCH *Gourmet Tofu Scramble*

IMPERIAL/METRIC		AMERICAN
2–3	spring onions (scallions)	2–3
2 tsp	vegan margarine	2 tsp
3–4 oz (85–115g)	tofu	⅓–½ cup
1 oz (30g)	vegan cream cheese	1 oz
¼ tsp	turmeric	¼ tsp
1 tsp	soya sauce	1 tsp
	freshly ground black pepper	
1 tbs	bacon-flavour soya bits	1 tbs
	wholemeal (whole wheat) toast	

1 Chop the spring onions (scallions) finely. Heat the margarine in a frying pan (skillet), and sauté them for 2–3 minutes.
2 Mash the tofu, vegan cream cheese, turmeric, and soya sauce together in a bowl. Grind in a little pepper.
3 Put the tofu mixture into the frying pan (skillet), and fry for a few minutes, stirring frequently.
4 Remove from the heat, stir in the bacon-flavour soya bits, and serve immediately over toast.

SUNDAY DINNER

Lentil and Mushroom-Stuffed Pancakes

IMPERIAL/METRIC		AMERICAN
	For the pancakes:	
1½ oz (45g)	wholemeal (whole wheat) flour	⅓ cup
1½ tsp	soya flour	1½ tsp
¼ tsp	baking powder	¼ tsp
pinch	sea salt	pinch
½ tsp	vegetable oil	½ tsp
as required	water	as required
as required	vegan margarine and/or vegetable oil for frying	as required
	For the filling:	
1 small	onion	1 small
1 clove	garlic	1 clove
2 tsp	vegan margarine	2 tsp
2 oz (55g)	mushrooms	1 cup
1½ oz (45g)	split red lentils	⅓ cup
¼ tsp	ground cumin seed	¼ tsp
4 fl oz (115ml)	water	½ cup
2 tsp	tomato paste	2 tsp
	sea salt and freshly ground black pepper to taste	
	For the sauce:	
1 tsp	vegan margarine	1 tsp
1 tsp	wholemeal (whole wheat) flour	⅓ cup
2½–3 fl oz (70–85ml)	soya milk	⅓ cup
½ oz (15g)	vegan hard cheese	½ oz

1   Mix the wholemeal (wholewheat) flour, soya flour, baking powder and salt in a bowl. Add the oil, then slowly add water, stirring all the while with a fork, until it has the texture of thick cream. Cover and leave to sit for at least half an hour.

2   Chop the onion. Crush the garlic. Heat the margarine in a saucepan, and sauté them for 2–3 minutes. Clean and chop the mushrooms finely. Add them to the pan and cook for another minute.

3   Wash and add the lentils, cumin and water. Bring to the boil, then lower the heat and simmer for 10–15 minutes.

4   Add the tomato paste and seasoning, cover the pan and leave to simmer for about 5 minutes longer, by which time the lentils should be cooked and the liquid absorbed.

5   Meanwhile, make the sauce by melting the margarine, stirring the flour in, and then gradually adding the milk until it is a smooth mixture. Grate the hard vegan cheese and stir it in.

6   Stir the pancake batter, and fry 4 small pancakes on both sides.

7   Fill the pancakes with the lentil mixture, and roll up or fold over. Spoon the sauce over the top. If using an oven then do this in an ovenproof dish; otherwise it can be done on a microwave-resistant plate that can also be eaten off.

8   Either bake at 350°F (180°C) Gas Mark 4 for 20–30 minutes, or microwave (uncovered) for 2 minutes.

SUNDAY DESSERT
Thai Banana Sweet

IMPERIAL/METRIC		AMERICAN
¼ 15 oz (420g) can	coconut milk	¼ 15 oz can
2 tsp	raw cane sugar	2 tsp
(or to taste)		(or to taste)
1	banana	1

1 Put the contents of the can into a liquidizer and blend thoroughly.
2 Pour a quarter into a small non-metallic bowl. (The remainder should be refrigerated for use later in the week.) Add the sugar, and microwave for 15 seconds. Stir. (Alternatively, put the ingredients into a small saucepan, and heat gently until warm.)
3 Slice the banana, and stir it in. Cover the bowl, and microwave for 1½ minutes, stirring halfway through. (Alternatively, add the banana to the saucepan, and cook until it has softened.) Serve hot.

MONDAY *Indonesian-style Green Curry*

IMPERIAL/METRIC		AMERICAN
2½–3 oz (70–85g)	brown rice	½ cup
2–3	spring onions (scallions)	2–3
1 clove	garlic	1 clove
1 small	fresh chilli	1 small
¼-inch	fresh ginger root	¼-inch
½ tsp	ground coriander	½ tsp
¼ tsp	ground cumin	¼ tsp
¼ tsp	turmeric	¼ tsp
¼ tsp	black pepper	¼ tsp
1 tbs	water	1 tbs
2 tsp	vegetable oil	2 tsp
¼ 15 oz (420g) can	coconut milk	¼ 15 oz can
	sea salt to taste	
5 oz (140g)	tofu	5 oz
2 tsp	vegan margarine	2 tsp

1 Put the rice on to cook.
2 Chop the spring onions (scallions), garlic, seeded chilli and peeled ginger, and put them in a blender. Add the spices and water and blend thoroughly.
3 Heat the oil in a saucepan and add the above mixture. Simmer uncovered over a low heat for 5–10 minutes, stirring occasionally.
4 Stir in the coconut milk and salt and continue simmering for a further 5–10 minutes.
5 Meanwhile, dice the tofu coarsely. Heat the margarine in a frying pan (skillet) and sauté the tofu until golden brown.
6 Stir the tofu into the coconut milk mixture, taste for seasoning, and serve over the rice.

TUESDAY *Middle-Eastern Beans*

IMPERIAL/METRIC		AMERICAN
1 small	onion	1 small
1 tbs	olive oil	1 tbs
1 clove	garlic	1 clove
1 small	fresh chilli	1 small
7 oz (200g) can	chopped tomatoes	7 oz can
½ 15 oz (420g) can	black-eyed beans (peas)	½ 15 oz can
2½–3 oz (70–85g)	couscous or bulgur wheat	½ cup

1　Chop the onion. Heat the oil in a saucepan, and stir in the onion. Crush the garlic and add it to the pan. Chop the chilli finely, and add it as well. Sauté these ingredients for about 3 minutes.
2　Stir in the tomatoes, bring to the boil, then lower the heat and leave to simmer for about 5 minutes.
3　Drain and rinse the beans. Add them to the pan, and simmer for a further 5 minutes.
4　Meanwhile, prepare the couscous or bulgur wheat, and serve the bean mixture over it.

WEDNESDAY *Spicy Oriental Noodles*

IMPERIAL/METRIC		AMERICAN
2½–3 oz (70–85g)	thin eggless noodles	2½–3 oz
2 oz (55g)	mushrooms	1 cup
2	spring onions (scallions)	2
2 oz (55g)	tofu	¼ cup
1 clove	garlic	1 clove
½-inch piece	fresh ginger root	½-inch piece
1 small	fresh chilli	1 small
1 tbs	vegetable oil	1 tbs
1 tsp	curry powder	1 tsp
2 oz (55g)	frozen peas	2 oz
¼ 15 oz (420g) can	coconut milk	¼ 15 oz can
2 tbs	soya sauce	2 tbs

1 Follow the instructions to cook or soak the noodles. Drain and set aside.
2 Slice the mushrooms. Chop the spring onions (scallions) and tofu finely. Set aside.
3 Chop the garlic, ginger and chilli finely. Heat the oil in a wok, and stir-fry for about 30 seconds.
4 Add the mushrooms, spring onions (scallions) and tofu to the wok. Stir-fry for a couple of minutes longer.
5 Stir in the curry powder, and stir-fry for about 20 seconds. Add the cooked noodles and peas to the wok and stir well. Stir in the coconut milk and soya sauce, and cook until everything is piping hot, and the liquid has evaporated.

THURSDAY *Pasta with Three (or Four) Cheeses*

IMPERIAL/METRIC		AMERICAN
3 oz (85g)	penne or rigatoni*	3 oz
1 oz (30g)	hard vegan cheese**	1 oz
2 tsp	vegan margarine	2 tsp
1 oz (30g)	vegan cream cheese	1 oz
2 tsp	vegan Parmesan	2 tsp
	freshly ground black pepper to taste	
	salad ingredients	

1 Cook the pasta until just tender. Drain and return to the warm pan.
2 Grate the hard cheese. Mix the margarine and cheeses into the pasta, and grind some pepper into the mixture.
3 Turn the mixture into a microwave-proof dish, cover and microwave for 2 minutes, stirring halfway through. Alternatively, turn it into a casserole dish and bake at 400°F (195°C) Gas Mark 6 for 10–15 minutes.
4 Serve accompanied with a green salad.

* A flavoured pasta works well in this dish.
** If you are able to get a range of vegan hard cheeses then use ½ oz (15g) each of 2 contrasting ones – e.g. Edam style and Cheddar style.

FRIDAY *Caribbean Rice and Beans*

IMPERIAL/METRIC		AMERICAN
2½–3 oz (70–85g)	brown rice	½ cup
1 small	onion	1 small
1 tbs	vegetable oil	1 tbs
¼–½-inch piece	fresh ginger root	¼–½-inch piece
1 small	fresh chilli	1 small
1 clove	garlic	1 clove
¼ 15 oz (420g) can	coconut milk	¼ 15 oz can
3–4 fl oz (75–115ml)	water	⅓–½ cup
¼ tsp	thyme	¼ tsp
	sea salt and freshly ground black pepper to taste	
½ 15 oz (420g) can	black-eyed beans (peas)	½ 15 oz can

1 If using rice from the health food stores that normally takes 30–45 minutes to cook, then cover it with boiling water in the morning and leave to soak all day; then drain and rinse. If using a quick-cook rice from the supermarket then simply rinse well.

2 Chop the onion. Heat the oil in a saucepan and sauté the onion for about 3 minutes.

3 Chop the ginger and chilli finely; crush the garlic. Add these to the saucepan, and fry for a couple of minutes longer.

4 Add the rice and stir-fry for a minute longer. Add the coconut milk, water (start with the lesser amount and add more if required during cooking), thyme and seasoning. Bring to the boil, then lower the heat, cover and simmer.

5 Drain and rinse the beans. After 15–20 minutes add the beans to the rice and cook for a few minutes longer until they are hot and all the liquid has been absorbed. Check for seasoning and serve immediately.

Indian Bread and Potato Cutlets

IMPERIAL/METRIC		AMERICAN
about 6 oz (170g)	potato	about 6 oz
1–2	spring onions (scallions)	1–2
2 slices	wholemeal (whole wheat) bread	2 slices
1 tsp	ground coriander	1 tsp
1 tsp	lemon juice	1 tsp
pinch	cayenne pepper or chilli powder	pinch
	sea salt to taste	
as required	vegetable oil	as required
as required	chutney	as required

1   Cook the potato until tender. Cool.
2   Chop the spring onions (scallions) finely.
3   Soak the bread in cold water for a couple of minutes and then squeeze out the water.
4   Peel the potato and mash it. Add the spring onions (scallions), bread, coriander, lemon juice, cayenne pepper or chilli powder and salt. Knead into a dough, and divide into 4 patties.
5   Heat a little oil in a frying pan (skillet), and shallow fry the cutlets until brown on both sides. (To make sure they are piping hot right through, they can be finished off in the microwave for about 30 seconds.) Serve with chutney.

Week 9

Shopping list

VEGETABLES AND FRUIT
Spring onions (scallions)
Small ripe avocado
Lemon
6 small onions
Celery
3 small carrots
Fresh ginger root
4 oz (115g) spinach
Small red pepper
Small courgette (zucchini)
2 oz (55g) mushrooms
1 large baking potato and
  1 small potato

MISCELLANEOUS
Tabasco sauce
Taco shells
Vegan 'turkey' or 'chicken'
  slices
Vegan mayonnaise
Cocoa powder
Chocolate sauce
Frozen peas
Tofu
Yellow split peas
Flaked (slivered) almonds
Tagliatelle
Vegan Worcestershire sauce

Check that you have all the staples listed on pages xiii and xiv.

Guacamole with Tacos

IMPERIAL/METRIC		AMERICAN
2	spring onions (scallions)	2
1 small	ripe avocado	1 small
2–3 tsp	lemon juice	2–3 tsp
1 tsp	olive oil	1 tsp
	Tabasco sauce to taste	
	sea salt and freshly ground	
	black pepper to taste	
4	taco shells	4

1 Chop the spring onions (scallions) finely.
2 Peel and mash the avocado coarsely, and stir in lemon juice, olive oil, Tabasco sauce, and seasoning.
3 Heat the taco shells according to the packet instructions and fill with guacamole.

SUNDAY DINNER
Baked Potato with 'Turkey' or 'Chicken' Hash

IMPERIAL/METRIC		AMERICAN
1 large	baking potato	1 large
1 small	onion	1 small
1 stick	celery	1 stick
3½ fl oz (100ml)	water	scant ½ cup
1 tbs	wholemeal (whole wheat) flour	1 tbs
additional	water	additional
2 tbs		2 tbs
1 tsp	yeast extract	1 tsp
2 oz (55g)	vegan 'turkey' or 'chicken' slices	2 oz
	sea salt and freshly ground black pepper to taste	
2 tsp	vegan margarine	2 tsp
2 tsp	soya cream	2 tsp

1 Clean and prick the potato, and put it in a hot oven to bake. (A potato cooked in a microwave oven will not have a pleasing texture at all, but it can be started or finished off in one to save time.)
2 Chop the onion and celery finely. Bring the water to the boil in a small saucepan, add these ingredients, and simmer, covered, over a low heat for a few minutes until just tender.
3 Mix the flour with the additional water in a cup, and stir it into the saucepan. Add the yeast extract.
4 Dice the vegan 'turkey' or 'chicken' and stir it into the saucepan. Simmer, uncovered, until piping hot, and season to taste.
5 Slice the potato in half, and with a fork mix in the margarine and cream. Pile the hash on top and serve immediately.

Hot Chocolate Pudding

IMPERIAL/METRIC		AMERICAN
1 oz (30g)	wholemeal (whole wheat) flour	¼ cup
½ tsp	baking powder	½ tsp
2 tsp	cocoa powder	2 tsp
1 oz (30g)	raw cane sugar	⅙ cup
¼ tsp	vanilla essence (extract)	¼ tsp
2 tsp	vegan mayonnaise	2 tsp
2 fl oz (55ml)	water	¼ cup
	chocolate sauce*	

1 Mix the flour, baking powder, cocoa powder and sugar together in a bowl (microwave-proof if microwaving it, or hotwater-proof if steaming it). Add the vanilla and mayonnaise, and stir in the water.

2 Cover the bowl with greaseproof (waxed) paper and microwave for 1½ minutes; leave to stand for 30 seconds. (Take great care in removing the bowl as it will be hot.) Alternatively, cover the bowl with foil or a lid, place it in a saucepan of simmering water, cover the saucepan, and steam over a low heat for 25 minutes.

3 Heat the sauce and pour it over the pudding.

* Most supermarkets have vegan chocolate sauces available.

MONDAY *'Turkey' or 'Chicken' Cacciatore*

IMPERIAL/METRIC		AMERICAN
1 small	onion	1 small
1 small	carrot	1 small
1 clove	garlic	1 clove
2 tsp	vegetable oil	2 tsp
1	bay leaf	1
4 fl oz (115ml)	water	½ cup
1 tbs	tomato paste	1 tbs
2 oz (55g)	frozen peas	2 oz
2½–3 oz (70–85g)	macaroni	2½–3 oz
2 oz (50g)	vegan 'turkey' or 'chicken' slices	2 oz
1 tbs	wholemeal (whole wheat) flour	1 tbs
as required	additional vegetable oil	as required
	sea salt and freshly ground black pepper to taste	

1 Skin and chop the onion, carrot and garlic. Heat the oil in a saucepan, and sauté the vegetables and bay leaf for 4–5 minutes.
2 Add the water and tomato paste to the pan, bring to the boil, then lower the heat, cover, and leave to simmer for about 5 minutes. Add the frozen peas, bring back to the boil and then simmer until just tender.
3 Cook the macaroni.
4 Dice the 'turkey' or 'chicken' slices. Spread the flour on a plate and toss the diced 'meat' in it, shaking off any flour that does not adhere.
5 Heat a little oil in a frying pan (skillet) and fry the diced 'meat' until lightly browned on both sides. Stir it into the sauce, season to taste, and serve it over the macaroni.

TUESDAY *Indian-Style Spinach with Tofu*

IMPERIAL/METRIC		AMERICAN
2½–3 oz (70–85g)	brown rice*	½ cup
4 oz (115g)	tofu**	½ cup
1 tbs	vegan margarine	1 tbs
	sea salt to taste	
1 small	onion	1 small
1 clove	garlic	1 clove
½-inch (1cm)	fresh ginger root	½-inch
2 tsp	vegetable oil	2 tsp
½ tsp	ground coriander seed	½ tsp
¼ tsp	turmeric	¼ tsp
¼ tsp	chilli powder	¼ tsp
4 oz (115g)	fresh spinach	4 oz
½ tsp	garam masala	½ tsp
	poppadum if required	

1 Put the rice on to cook.
2 Drain, dry and dice the tofu into ½-inch (1cm) cubes. Heat the margarine in a frying pan (skillet), and shallow-fry the tofu cubes until golden. Remove from the pan and drain on a kitchen (paper) towel. Sprinkle with sea salt.
3 Chop the onion. Crush the garlic. Peel and grate the ginger. Heat the vegetable oil in a saucepan, and sauté these ingredients until beginning to brown. Stir in the spices and cook for a minute or so longer.
4 Chop the spinach coarsely and wash if unwashed. Add it to the saucepan with 1 tbs of water. Stir into the onion and spice mixture, lower the heat, cover the pan and cook until just tender.
5 Add the tofu cubes to the pan, raise the heat and cook until the mixture is dry. Sprinkle with garam masala and serve over rice.

* If making the whole week's menus, then cook twice as much rice, and cool and refrigerate half.
** If making the whole week's menus, then freeze 5–6 oz (140–170g) tofu.

WEDNESDAY *Spaghetti with Red Lentil Sauce*

IMPERIAL/METRIC		AMERICAN
1 small	onion	1 small
1 clove	garlic	1 clove
½ small	red pepper	½ small
2 tsp	olive oil	2 tsp
1½ oz (45g)	split red lentils	⅓ cup
¼ pint (150ml)	water	⅔ cup
1 tbs	tomato paste	1 tbs
	sea salt and freshly ground black pepper to taste	
3 oz (85g)	wholemeal (whole wheat) spaghetti	3 oz
	vegan Parmesan (optional)	

1. Peel the onion and garlic; de-seed the pepper. Chop these ingredients finely.
2. Heat the oil in a saucepan and sauté the vegetables for about 3 minutes.
3. Wash and add the lentils to the saucepan. Stir in the water and tomato paste, bring to the boil, lower the heat, cover the pan, and simmer for about 15 minutes until the lentils are tender and the liquid is absorbed. Season to taste.
4. Meanwhile, cook the spaghetti, drain it, and serve it with the sauce, sprinkled with vegan Parmesan if desired.

THURSDAY *Lemon Vegetable Rice with a Middle-Eastern Flavour*

IMPERIAL/METRIC		AMERICAN
1 small	onion	1 small
1 small	courgette (zucchini)	1 small
1 small	carrot	1 small
½ small	red pepper	½ small
½ oz (15g)	vegan margarine	1 tbs
juice and rind of		juice and rind of
½ small	lemon	½ small
2½–3 oz (70–85g)	brown rice, cooked	½ cup
½ tsp	cinnamon	½ tsp
¼ tsp	grated nutmeg	¼ tsp
	sea salt and freshly ground black pepper to taste	
1 oz (30g)	toasted flaked (slivered) almonds	¼ cup

1 Slice the onion thinly. Cut the courgette (zucchini) into ¼-inch (6mm) slices. Slice the carrot into matchsticks and the red pepper into thin strips.
2 Heat the margarine in a largish frying pan (skillet) or saucepan, and sauté the vegetables for about 3 minutes over a medium heat.
3 Add the lemon juice and rind, lower the heat, cover the pan, and leave to cook for about 3 minutes longer.
4 Add the rice, cinnamon, nutmeg and seasoning, and stir over a medium heat until it is all piping hot.
5 Stir in the nuts and serve immediately.

FRIDAY *Peanutty Tofu Chunks on Tagliatelle with Mushroom Topping*

IMPERIAL/METRIC		AMERICAN
5–6 oz (140–170g)	frozen tofu	⅔ cup
1 tbs	peanut butter	1 tbs
3 tsp	vegetable oil	3 tsp
2 tsp	soya sauce	2 tsp
1 tbs plus	water	1 tbs plus
4 fl oz (115ml)		½ cup
1 clove	garlic	1 clove
3 oz (85g)	eggless tagliatelle	3 oz
2 oz (55g)	mushrooms	1 cup
1 tsp	cornflour (cornstarch)	1 tsp
1 tbs	vegan Worcestershire sauce	1 tbs

1 Thaw the tofu, squeeze out any moisture, and dice it. Set aside.
2 In a bowl mix the peanut butter, 1 tsp oil, soya sauce, and 1 tbs water. Crush the garlic and stir it into the mixture.
3 Stir the frozen tofu chunks into the peanut butter mixture until they are thoroughly coated. Heat the oven to 375°F (190°C) Gas Mark 5. Put the coated tofu chunks onto a baking sheet, and bake for 10 minutes; flip them over and cook for a further 10 minutes.
4 Meanwhile, cook the tagliatelle according to the packet instructions.
5 Slice the mushrooms and sauté them in the remaining oil until lightly browned. In a cup whisk the cornflour (cornstarch) into the 4 fl oz (½ cup) water, and stir in the Worcestershire sauce. Stir this into the mushrooms and simmer briefly.
6 Drain the tagliatelle, put the tofu chunks on top, and spoon the mushroom sauce over this. Serve immediately.

SATURDAY LUNCH French Split Pea and Vegetable Soup

IMPERIAL/METRIC		AMERICAN
1 oz (30g)	yellow split peas	¼ cup
¾ pint (420ml)	boiling water	2 cups
1 small	onion	1 small
1 small	potato	1 small
1 small	carrot	1 small
1 stick	celery	1 stick
¼ tsp	dried marjoram	¼ tsp
¼ tsp	dried thyme	¼ tsp
¼ tsp	dried oregano	¼ tsp
1 small	bay leaf	1 small
1 tsp	vegan margarine	1 tsp
	sea salt and freshly ground black pepper to taste	

1　First thing in the morning (or the night before if preferred) wash the split peas, place them in a saucepan, cover with boiling water, and leave to stand.
2　When ready to prepare lunch, peel and chop the onion finely; wash and chop the potato, carrot and celery finely.
3　Bring the saucepan with the split peas to the boil, add the finely chopped vegetables and the herbs; lower the heat, cover the pan, and leave to simmer for about 20 minutes, by which time all the vegetables should be tender.
4　Remove the bay leaf. Stir in the margarine and season to taste. Serve accompanied with bread, toast, crackers or oatcakes.

Index